FAVORITE OBJECT
TALKS

by

Joseph A. Schofield, Jr.

BAKER BOOK HOUSE
Grand Rapids, Michigan

ISBN: 0-8010-8017-7

Taken from
53 Object Sunday Talks to Children

PHOTOLITHOPRINTED BY CUSHING - MALLOY, INC.
ANN ARBOR, MICHIGAN, UNITED STATES OF AMERICA
1973

Preface

Most preachers and teachers who use objects when talking to boys and girls are torn between two ideals. Shall they employ elaborate and complicated objects—showy and impressive—yet foreign to the child's experience? Or shall they use common things, things the child sees and perhaps uses every day, things certainly with which he is entirely familiar, and draw spiritual lessons from objects daily handled and observed? In the first case, the lesson must be elaborately drawn out of elaborate material and it is often very difficult to make the reasoning clear and the lesson apparent. In the second case, the object may be so familiar that the child's attention is not arrested and strongly held by curiosity and a new sense of interest.

Nevertheless, it seems to me that the second method has the distinct advantage of starting at a point quite within the child's experience and the spiritual lessons drawn can be clear, simple and vivid. There is another great advantage in using familiar objects. The speaker can easily acquire them—usually he has only to pick them up in his own study or household—and he does not need to engage in detailed and elaborate mechanical preparation. And most teachers and preachers are not mechanics!

Mostly the second method has been employed in this book of talks based on objects. Only a few of the objects suggested require any detailed preparation and I have tried to give explicit directions in these cases. Many of the subjects treated in this book were originally suggested to me by the children of my congregation (and some of the older folks, too) who, in response to my request, told me of objects or themes around which they would like to hear me build Children's Sermons. Many of the themes proposed were very suggestive. Often one of them presented a challenge—not to say a dare—to the preacher's ingenuity. But all of them, even the simplest and the most absurd, being as they were entirely familiar to the children, presented distinct opportunities to draw spiritual lessons.

I want here to reiterate my profound conviction that children can understand the Gospel. It need not be toned down or excused or explained away or glossed over or just plainly ignored for their benefit. Too many teachers to-day, enamored by the modern emphasis of the "latest pedagogical experts" on adapting teaching methods and teaching materials to age-groups and presenting to children only so much of truth as they can readily assimilate, fall into the grave error of so reducing the Christian message as to ignore its heart and even, in places, deny its truth. These talks are frankly intended to be vitally Christian. The basic truths of Christ's deity, the inspiration of God's Word, the need for salvation, God's gracious provision of it through Jesus Christ, His Son, can and should be presented to children. To withhold these truths from them is a betrayal of trust. I pray that these talks may help others do what I for years have been endeavoring to do, preach Christ and Him crucified to little children for whom, as for the whole world, He died.

J. A. S., Jr.

Gouverneur, New York

Contents

Contents

A New Year

(NEW YEAR SUNDAY)

JOSHUA 3:4: ". . . ye have not passed this way heretofore."

OBJECT: A calendar of the old year. Tear off the last leaf—December.

TO-DAY is a great day. It is the first Sunday in the New Year. It is New Year's Sunday, in other words.

I have an old calendar here, a calendar of the year that has just ended. You see that December is on the last leaf. When I tear off this last leaf we show that the year is gone as well as the month whose page I removed. When this last page of the calendar is removed, not only has a new month started, but also a new year. You even have to begin with a new calendar altogether. For the new year has come. The new year has begun. Let us talk about A New Year.

And let us use a text from God's Word. I am going to read to you the last part of a verse that is found in the Book of Joshua, the 3rd chapter and the 4th verse. ". . . ye have not passed this way heretofore."

The Children of Israel were about to cross over the Jordan River and enter into the Promised Land, under Joshua, their new, great leader. It was a new and wonderful experience for them. They were entering into a new land. They were entering into a new and different kind of life. Everything would be different. Everything would be new. And they were told to remember that. ". . . ye have not passed this way heretofore."

We are going into a new year. Everything will be different. Everything will be new. For we have not passed this way heretofore.

Some one has said, "To-day is the to-morrow you looked forward to yesterday." Had you ever thought how true that is, boys and girls? To-day is the to-morrow you looked forward to yesterday. Yesterday you waited for to-morrow. Well, to-morrow is here. Only we now call it to-day.

Longfellow, the great American poet, once wrote:

> "Nothing that is can pause or stay;
> The moon will wax, the moon will wane,
> The mist and cloud will turn to rain,
> The rain to mist and cloud again,
>   To-morrow be to-day." *

When to-morrow gets here, it will be to-day.

The same thing is true with a year. When next year gets here, it will be this year. We can never recall the year that is gone. We can never get it back. It is gone forever.

But a new year is ahead of us, a whole new year. We have not used any of it up yet. It is all there ahead of us to use. When *it* is gone, we cannot recall it either. So let us make the most of it while we have it. Let us not

* Keramos

waste it. Let us not throw it away. Let us not destroy it. Let us get the very most we can out of it.

I

Let us make the new year that is ahead of us a New Year of Kindness. We can, you know, if we try hard enough. We can make it a whole year of kindness. The Bible says, you remember, ". . . be ye kind one to another." *

II

And let us make it a New Year of Love. The whole year that stretches out in front of us ought to be a year of love. We can make it a year of love if we want to hard enough and if we try hard enough and if we ask God to help us often enough. Let us determine that we shall make it a year of love. For Christ Himself commanded us, you know, ". . . love one another; as I have loved you." ** Christ has commanded it. Let us do it.

III

And, finally, let us make it a New Year of Obedience to Christ. If we do that, it will be a fine new year. If we do that, it will be truly a Happy New Year. For after all, there is nothing finer that we can do and nothing more important than to obey Christ in all that we do, in all that we plan, in all that we say, in all that we think. To obey Christ is the highest duty of life, boys and girls. To obey Christ is the greatest joy in life. Remember how Christ said to us, "Follow me." *** That means go where

* Ephesians 4:32
** John 13:34
*** John 1:43

He wants us to go; do what He wants us to do; say what He wants us to say; think what He wants us to think. "Follow me," Jesus said. That means obey Him. Let us not forget that. For that will make the new year a Happy New Year.

2

Abraham Lincoln and His Mother*

(LINCOLN'S BIRTHDAY)

❧ ☙

OBJECT: A picture of Abraham Lincoln.

❧ ☙

WE CELEBRATE Abraham Lincoln's birthday this week. Lincoln was the greatest American and we all are proud to remember his birthday. I want to tell you something about Lincoln and his mother this morning, for his mother had much to do with his greatness. Indeed, once he said, "All that I am, or hope to be, I owe to my angel mother. I remember my mother's prayers, and they have always followed me." Here is the story of Lincoln's first great sorrow.

"Abraham," the voice came from the little cot and could hardly be heard. For on this cot lay a young wife and mother dying, sacrificing her young and lovely life 'way out in the back woods. The cot was in a tiny "shack" of a pioneer, deep in the woods. There were no windows to the tiny house and the doors stood open to the sunlight which danced on the floor of tramped earth. The furniture was very little and very crude, just a few stools made out of rough boards and no chairs. There were a few dishes but there was no cupboard.

---

* This sermon is based on "Lincoln's First Great Sorrow" as told by Hezikiah Butterworth and retold by the late Rev. Louis Albert Banks. My sincere thanks go to Mrs. Banks for her kind permission to use it here.

"What is it?" the young boy answered with an anxious tone in his voice as he hurried to her side. Lifting up her feeble arms, the dying woman drew her son to herself and spoke to him with a voice full of love and hope.

"I am going to leave you, Abe—and—oh, how hard it is to part with you! How beautiful it is outdoors! It is beautiful wherever God is, and I am going to meet Him in a brighter world than this. I learned to love him at the old camp meetings, and I want you to learn to love Him, too.

"I have not had much to make me happy—far less than some folks have had—but my voice has never failed to rise in praise whenever a feeling of thanksgiving has come to me.

"Abraham Lincoln, you have my heart. I am thankful God gave you to us. Love everybody; hinder nobody, and the world will be glad, some day, that you were born. This is a beautiful world, to the loving and believing. I am grateful for life; for everything, but, more than all else, because you have my heart."

"But he can't sing, Nancy!" A tall pioneer in buckskin stood in the cabin doorway. He had just stepped to the door and had heard the conversation. He saw death creeping into the room and knew his loved wife would not have long for this world. So he added a gentle laugh to his joking words for he wanted to cheer his dying wife even in the last few minutes of her life. She said nothing, and so her husband repeated his little joke, with love and laughter in his voice.

"But he can't sing like you, Nancy."

"The heart sings in many ways," she answered, very feebly. "Some hearts make other hearts sing. Abraham may not have my voice, but he has my heart, and he may make others sing. I am going, now." And with these words, she turned her head toward the split logs that made the wall of the little house. Her fingers played nervously over the covers of the cot; she opened and closed her eyes; once or twice she said, ever so softly, "My Abraham!" Once she tried to lift herself to see him again. Once she trembled. And then she was still.

"She's gone, Ab'ram!" The father's voice was gentle.

With their own hands, the father and son made her coffin. And together they buried her beneath the trees. Young Abraham had nothing to say. His heart was filled with sorrow and sadness. He had known hardship and suffering. He had known privation and want. But this was almost too much for him to bear. And always, through his entire life, he remembered his mother and remembered, too, that he had her heart.

Abraham Lincoln did make other hearts to sing, just as his mother said he would. The world was indeed glad that he was born. He had his mother's heart. It was his mother who made him great.

3

Love's Day

(VALENTINE'S DAY)

MATTHEW 22:37-39: "Jesus said unto him, Thou shalt love the Lord thy God with all thy heart, and with all thy soul, and with all thy mind. This is the first and great command-

ment. And the second is like unto it, Thou shalt love thy
neighbor as thyself."

JOHN 3:16: "For God so loved the world, that he gave his only
begotten Son, that whosoever believeth in him should not
perish, but have everlasting life."

OBJECTS: A valentine for display and a quantity of cardboard
valentines with lollipops attached to give to each child at
the end of the service.

I HAVE two texts for the boys and girls this morning.
You know I think most sermons should have texts,
whether sermons to grown-ups or sermons to children.
And the text is a good place to begin. So I am beginning
this morning with two texts. Maybe that will make the
sermon twice as good. What do you think?

Well, here are the two texts. One is from God's Book,
from the Gospel according to Matthew, the 22nd chapter and the 37th to 39th verses. "Jesus said unto him,
Thou shalt love the Lord thy God with all thy heart,
and with all thy soul, and with all thy mind. This is the
first and great commandment. And the second is like
unto it, Thou shalt love thy neighbor as thyself." The
other text is also from God's Book, from the Gospel
according to John, the 3rd chapter and the 16th verse.
"For God so loved the world, that he gave his only begotten Son, that whosoever believeth in him should not
perish, but have everlasting life."

And I have an object for the Children's Sermon this
morning, too. You know what it is as I hold it up before
you in my hand. Certainly, it is a valentine. After the
service, I am going to give each child present a valentine
with a lollipop attached to it.

For Valentine's Day comes this week. Now Valentine's Day is a day on which we think of *love*. That's the day when we think of love. And it is *right* and *proper* that we should think of love on Valentine's Day. For, after all, Valentine's Day is *Love's Day*.

We love one another and we should. So why should we not think about it once in a while? Surely Valentine's Day is a proper day on which to think of love. We love one another. That's right and proper. We ought to, certainly. But let us not forget our parents. We should love them, too, shouldn't we? And not just one day a year, either. Let us love our parents on Valentine's Day and every day. That is right. That is as it should be.

But let us also remember to love God. And that not on one day a year only, either. Let us not forget to love God. We should love Him on Valentine's Day, too, should we not? But our love to God is not meant for just one day. We should love Him every day.

Now right here is where Christ's two great commandments come in. The first of our two texts is Matthew 22: 37-39. "Jesus said unto him, Thou shalt love the Lord thy God with all thy heart, and with all thy soul, and with all thy mind. This is the first and great commandment. And the second is like unto it, Thou shalt love thy neighbor as thyself." We are told that we ought to love God with all our heart. That's a Valentine text, isn't it? And we are told to love our neighbor as ourselves. That's a Valentine text, too. Christ commanded us to love; to love God, to love each other.

But why should we love God? We love God because He first loved us.*

How much did He love us? That question brings us

* 1 John 4:19.

to our second text. And here we find the answer. John 3:16. "For God so loved the world, that he gave his only begotten Son, that whosoever believeth in him should not perish, but have everlasting life."

(Cardboard valentines with lollipops attached may be given to each child as he leaves the Church.)

4

Our First Citizen

(WASHINGTON'S BIRTHDAY)

1 SAMUEL 9:2: "And he had a son, whose name was Saul, a choice young man, and a goodly: and there was not among the children of Israel a goodlier person than he: from his shoulders and upward he was higher than any of the people."

OBJECTS: Small American flags to be given to each child as the children leave the Church for Junior Church or at the end of the service.

I HAVE a text for the boys and girls this morning. It is found in God's Word, the Bible, in the First Book of Samuel, the 9th chapter and the 2nd verse. "And he had a son, whose name was Saul, a choice young man, and a goodly: and there was not among the children of Israel a goodlier person than he: from his shoulders and upward he was higher than any of the people." This text described Saul, the first King of Israel. It says that Saul was a choice young man, and a goodly. It says that there was not a finer young man in all of Israel. And it goes on to say that Saul was tall, taller than all the men in the country. A fine young man, tall, brave, handsome, good. There was no better, no grander, no finer in all the land. That was Saul, the first King of Israel. The text speaks of him.

But that same text could be applied very well indeed to George Washington, the first President of the United States, whose birthday comes this week. For he, too, was a choice young man, and a goodly. There was not in the whole country a finer man than he. And he, too, like Saul, was tall and stately, and handsome and brave and good. There was no better, no grander, no finer young man in all the land. So the same text that describes Saul, the first King of Israel, will also describe George Washington, the first President of the United States.

George Washington was our first citizen. Surely, he was one of our greatest men. He was the founder of our nation. We call him the Father of our Country. I call him "Our First Citizen."

Some one said something like that of him once. It was Representative Henry Lee, a Congressman in our National Capital. This is the way he put it about George Washington. He said he was "first in war, first in peace, and first in the hearts of his countrymen."

What did he mean by that? "First in war; first in peace; first in the hearts of his countrymen." Well, this is what he meant, I think.

George Washington was the leader, the first man in war. George Washington was the leader, the first man in peace. George Washington was the leader, thought most of, in the hearts of his countrymen. He was the chief man, the general, the boss, the head, in time of war. He was the chief man, the general, the boss, the head of the nation, in times of peace. And he was the chief man, the general, the boss, the head of the people, in their hearts. He was the leading man in war. He was the leading man in peace. He was the leading man in men's hearts.

The first in war was Washington; the others followed. The first in peace was Washington; the others followed. The first in the hearts of the people was Washington; the others loved him and followed him.

We should follow in his steps, *Our First Citizen's* steps, as he tried to follow Jesus!

I have a small flag for each member of the Junior Congregation this morning. The ushers will give them to you and I ask you to hold them high as you march down the aisle to shake my hand and then on to Junior Church.

5

*Pennies and Dimes**

(CANVASS SUNDAY)

1 CORINTHIANS 16:2: "Upon the first day of the week let every one of you lay by him in store, as God hath prospered him, that there be no gatherings when I come."

* As usual, the help of my wife, Mary Lewis Schofield, has been invaluable in getting this volume of talks to children ready for publication. I cannot begin to thank her for her many services nor for the encouragement and numerous suggestions she has always given me. But just here I do want to acknowledge the suggestions from her that became the bases of Chapters V and IX.

OBJECT: A Church offering envelope.

TO-DAY is Canvass Sunday. This afternoon some of your fathers will visit every home in the congregation to ask the people of our Church how much they will promise to pay to keep the Church going this next year and how much they will promise to give so that people all over the world may hear of Christ. I have a boys' and girls' text for Canvass Sunday. It is found in God's Book, in the First letter to the Corinthians, the 16th chapter and the 2nd verse. "Upon the first day of the week let every one of you lay by him in store, as God hath prospered him, that there be no gatherings when I come."

And here is an offering envelope, the kind our people use every Sunday to give their gifts to the Church and to missions. What they want to give to our Church they put in the black side of the envelope. What they want to give to missions they put in the red side.

And now I have a true story for you. The other day a little boy I know was making some change. He was getting ready to go on an errand and he was looking his money over to see, I suppose, if he had enough. He was looking at the different pieces of money in his hand, naming them over and figuring out what each one was worth, what each one would buy and how much they were worth when they were all put together. I think he must have had some pennies and some nickels and some dimes in his hand. And maybe a quarter or two, besides. This one was a penny, he would say. This one was a nickel. This one was a dime. And then he said, "The pennies go to Church. The dimes go to the show."

There was a lot of truth in what he said. Too often it is true that the pennies go to Church and the dimes go to the show. Too often it is true that all of us spend much more on our pleasures than we do on our religion.

"Pennies go to Church. Dimes go to the show." That made me think.

I

And the first thing it made me think of was this. The greatest thing on earth costs nothing. That is important. The greatest thing on earth costs nothing. *Salvation is free.* The Bible says, ". . . without money and without price." * So salvation is free. But the Church that tells us of it must be kept up. The Church that tells people about God and about His salvation must be lighted and heated and maintained. That takes money. But it need not cost much if all will do their part.

II

And the second thing it made me think of is this. We value what we pay for. Things that cost us little or nothing we are apt to think of as worth little or nothing. The things that we get without effort we often do not value. Things that we have not paid for we frequently think are not worth taking care of. Once we know how much a thing is worth because we have paid for it ourselves, perhaps working hard to earn the money, then we appreciate it and realize that it is valuable and understand how truly important it is. You will think more of the Church and the Sunday School if you give to support them. They will be more and more *your* Church and Sunday School if you give to them. If you help *pay* for them, you will respect them more, you

* Isaiah 55:1

will value them more, you will appreciate them more, you will enjoy them more.

III

And the third thing I want to say is that everybody should support the Church. Everybody who benefits from the Church should support the Church. *Everybody*. The boys and girls should do their share. The boys and girls should have a very definite part in supporting the Church. It belongs to them as well as to the grown-ups. Every boy and every girl, then, ought to have a part in keeping the Church going. Every boy and every girl should give to the Church. Each should do his share. Here is our text, I am sure. 1 Corinthians 16:2. "Upon the first day of the week let every one of you lay by him in store, as God hath prospered him, that there be no gatherings when I come." Do you notice what this text says?

1

We are to give regularly. "Upon the *first day of the week*." That means each week, every week, regularly on a certain day of the week, the first day of the week. We are to give right along, every week, in regular fashion. The Church envelope helps us do this. For there is an envelope for each Sunday and each one is dated. This reminds us to put our money in it every week. And if we forget one week, we can make it up the next. And there is also a place in the envelope for what we give to the Church here at home and a separate place in the double envelope for what we want to give to missions.

2

Then the text says next that *all are to give.* "*Every one of you.*" Not just father or mother or sister or brother. Not just one for a family or one for a street or one for a neighborhood. But every one is to give. I hope every member of every family in our Church will have a set of Church envelopes and use them regularly. If you do not have a set, ask the Church Treasurer for one!

3

And finally the text says that we are to give *as much as we can.* Here is the way it reads: ". . . *as God hath prospered him.*" That means we are to give as much as we can, as much as we are able, as God has helped us, as God has prospered us. That is the way the Bible says to give to the Church. That is the way God asks it. That is the way God wants it.

6

"In Remembrance of Me"

(COMMUNION)

LUKE 22:19: ". . . this do in remembrance of me."

OBJECTS: A piece of communion bread and a cup of communion wine.

To-DAY is Communion Sunday and later on in this service the members of the Church will take Communion. Christ told us to have Communion. He said so in our text this morning, Luke 22:19, the last part of the verse: ". . . this do in remembrance of me."

When we join the Church, boys and girls, we will take Communion, too. But I think it is a good idea to think about it even before we become Church members so that we will understand it even better when we do. So, even though the boys and girls this morning are not going to take Communion (as we say) and even though they are off in another part of the Church building having Junior Church during the serving of Communion to the grown-ups, I think they ought to know a little about Communion and understand why we have it. When they are old enough to take it, too, they will appreciate it all the more.

Here are the two elements that the Church members will be taking when they come in a few moments to the Communion Service. Here is some bread that they will eat. And here is some grape juice in little cups that they will drink. Now why are they going to eat this little bit of bread and drink this little bit of grape juice? Because Christ told them to. And why did He tell them to? To remember Him. That is the purpose of Communion. That is the command Christ gave us in our text. "This do in remembrance of me." We have Communion to remember Christ.

I

First of all, we remember Who He is. When your fathers and mothers take this bread and drink from this cup, they remember Christ, Who He is. He is God's Son. We are to remember that. That is most important. We remember that Jesus Christ is the Son of God.

II

Then, next, we remember what He did. The Communion helps us remember that Christ died for us. The

cross is the symbol of our religion. For every time we
see a cross we are to remember that Christ, our Lord
and Master, died on a cross for us. And every time a
friend of Jesus takes the bread of the Communion and
drinks the juice of the grape which is in the Communion cup, he remembers that Christ died for us.

III

But if we remember what He did for us, we are also
to remember in the Communion service what He does
for us. Do you notice the difference in these two words
that I have used? We remember what Christ *did*. But
we also are to remember what Christ *does*. He did everything for us one day so many years ago. But He is doing
something for us every day of our lives besides. Christ
loved us so much that He died for us. But He still loves
us so much that He is doing things for us every day and
all day and all the time.

He is always at our side. He is our best Friend. He is
our Guide. He leads us along the way, into the right
way, into the best way. He is our Shepherd. He cares
for us, He protects us, He shields us, He leads us, He
feeds us, He provides for us, He looks after us. He is our
Shepherd. He is our Helper, our great Helper.

IV

Then we are to remember, also, that He comes to us
in the Communion. Now that may at first be hard for
us to understand. But think a moment and you will see
what I mean. Jesus can live in your heart, can't He?
You know whether or not Jesus is living in your heart.
And in a very special way Jesus comes into our hearts
in the Communion service. When the Church members

eat this bread and drink this juice, Jesus comes to them. That's the wonderful thing about it! Jesus wants to live in our hearts. And He comes to us, especially in this service we call Communion.

V

And besides all this, we remember that we give our-selves to Him, especially in the Communion service. He comes to us. He lives in our hearts. He wants to live in our hearts. But He also wants us to give ourselves to Him. And if He comes to us especially in the Com-munion, He asks and He wants and He expects us to give ourselves to Him, especially in the Communion.

And so in Communion we remember Him. For He said to us, ". . . this do in remembrance of me."

7

Palms or Garments or Hearts?

(PALM SUNDAY)

MATTHEW 21:8, 15: "And a very great multitude spread their garments in the way; others cut down branches from the trees, and strawed them in the way. . . . And when the chief priests and scribes saw the wonderful things that he did, and the children crying in the temple, and saying, Hosanna to the son of David; they were sore displeased."

OBJECTS: A branch of a palm tree; a loose robe or similar garment to give the effect of a garment worn in Jesus' day; a heart cut from cardboard.

I HAVE with me in the pulpit this morning three objects that I want to show to the boys and girls. Here is a palm branch. And here is a loose garment something like the coats or outer coverings people wore when Jesus was on earth. And here is a piece of cardboard cut out to look like a heart. I have a palm; a garment; a heart.

You all heard, I am sure, because you all listen to the Scripture reading carefully, the story of Palm Sunday as it was read in Church this morning. And you all have noticed the beautiful palm buds with which the Church is decorated to-day. Of course, it is Palm Sunday. So we read the Palm Sunday Scripture. And we have palms in Church for decoration.

But now I want to read to you your own special texts,

two of them, in fact. First, Matthew 21:8. "And a very great multitude spread their garments in the way; others cut down branches from the trees, and strawed them in the way." This text tells us something that happened on the first Palm Sunday. Many people took their coats off their backs and spread them on the ground for Jesus to ride over as He came into Jerusalem that day. And many other people cut down branches off the palm trees, and spread them before Him. And the second text is Matthew 21:15. "And when the chief priests and scribes saw the wonderful things that he did, and the children crying in the temple, and saying, Hosanna to the son of David; they were sore displeased." This verse tells us something that happened on Monday, the day after Palm Sunday. On Monday, Jesus did many wonderful things; the children cried out in the Temple and shouted praise and glory to Jesus; and the chief priests and the scribes were very much displeased.

I

Now just notice the three things that these verses tell us people gave to Jesus on Palm Sunday and on Monday, the day following.

1

Some gave palms. "Others cut down branches from the trees, and strawed them in the way." Palm trees grew everywhere in that country. So many people cut branches off the palm trees and cast them in the road for the little donkey, on which Christ rode, to walk over. They just cut branches from the trees and made a carpet for Jesus to ride upon. They gave Him palms that cost them nothing.

2

And some gave garments. They loved Jesus, too, and they wanted to give Him something to show they loved Him. So they took their coats off their backs and cast them into the road for Him to ride upon. "A very great multitude spread their garments in the way." This cost these people a lot. They were wearing good clothes, without a doubt. But they wanted to join in making a lovely, soft carpet for their King to ride over, so they freely gave to Him their clothes.

3

And still others gave their hearts. "The children crying in the temple, and saying, Hosanna to the son of David." They were praising Him. They were shouting their love. They were giving Him their hearts; and their hearts were really everything they had.

So some gave palms that cost nothing. Some gave garments that cost a great deal. Some gave their hearts, everything they had.

But notice this especially. Some who gave palms, even some who gave garments, never really gave Him their hearts. For they shouted, "Crucify Him" on Friday.

II

Now you know Christ expects us to give to Him. Just as He expected those people of Palm Sunday to give things to Him, so He expects us. Not just on Palm Sunday, of course; but every Sunday; and not just on Sunday, of course, but every day and all the time.

1

He expects us to *give Him palms*. I mean nature's gifts. I mean flowers from our gardens, songs and praises. Maybe we can do some work for Him and thus give Him work. Certainly we can give Him time; at least the time we spend in Sunday School and in Church. These gifts may not cost us very much. They may cost us nothing at all. *But Christ accepts them all if we really mean it when we give.*

2

Then Christ also expects us to *give garments.* I do not mean the clothes you wear to Church and Sunday School. But I do mean things that cost us something, just as those garments thrown down in the Jerusalem street that first Palm Sunday cost their owners something. We can give to Christ things that are worth something, things that cost something. We can give to Church and Sunday School. And Christ expects us to. We can give to the Church for its upkeep and its work. We can give to spread missions. We can give to start Sunday Schools in places where boys and girls have none at all now. We surely can give to Christ by giving to His Church. *Every child should have a Church envelope* and put something in it every single week. Certainly we should give to God. *And Christ accepts it if we really mean it when we give.*

3

And also, never forget, Christ expects us to *give Him our hearts.* Indeed that is what Christ wants most of all. *Yes, that is what He really wants. Give your hearts to Him, all of you. For Christ accepts them if we really mean it when we give.*

8

The First Day of the Week

(EASTER)

❦

JOHN 20:1: "The first day of the week cometh Mary Magdalene
early, when it was yet dark, unto the sepulchre, and seeth
the stone taken away from the sepuchre."

OBJECT: A calendar of the current month showing the Sundays
in red.

❦

I WANT to read to the boys and girls this morning a
text from God's Word. It is the 1st verse of the 20th
chapter of the Gospel according to John. "The first day
of the week cometh Mary Magdalene early, when it
was yet dark, unto the sepulchre, and seeth the stone
taken away from the sepulchre." Now that is the beginning of the Easter story as John tells it. On the first day
of the week, that's Sunday, Mary Magdalene came to
the tomb and found it empty. You notice that this text
says it all happened on *the first day of the week*. I want
also to show you this page from the calendar showing
the present month. Won't you notice, please, how the
Sundays, the first day of each week, are marked in red?

Now the day we call Sunday is the first day of the
week. It comes first in every week. But it is also the most
important day in every week. So we call Sunday the
"First" day for that reason, too. It is first in time. It
is the first day that comes in every week. And it is first

in importance. It is the most important day of the week.

But why is it so important? Why is Sunday first in importance as well as first in time? Why, because Christ rose from the dead on a Sunday! That's what makes Sunday the most important day in every week and Easter Sunday the most important day in every year! Christ rose on Sunday. And because Christ rose, we will live forever. Think of that! Because Christ rose on Easter Sunday, many years ago, we, you and I and all His people, shall live *forever!* More than that, and listen to this carefully, because Christ once rose from the dead, we are going some day to rise from the dead, too! Does that not tell you why Sunday is so important and why Easter Sunday is the most important day of all the year?

So you see, with Sunday so important, and with Sunday coming once a week, we really celebrate Christ's resurrection *every week*. We do not need to wait for Easter to come around once a year. We can and we really do celebrate Christ's resurrection every week, every Sunday. That is really and truly what Sunday means and ought to mean to us all. Before this, that is before Christ arose on the first Easter Sunday, the Jews (God's people) worshipped God on the seventh day of the week. But after this, that is after Christ's resurrection on the first Easter Sunday, Christ's followers (God's people) worshipped God on the first day of the week.

Therefore we should remember on *every* Sunday that Christ arose. That is what Sunday really means. Remember on *every* Sunday that Christ is alive. That is what Sunday should mean to us. Come to Church *every* Sunday (not just once a year) to show that we love Christ and want to worship Him. Every Sunday (don't you see?) is a sort of Easter. Every Sunday is an anniversary of Christ's resurrection. Every Sunday is a day upon which we ought to gather together to praise Him, to worship Him, to thank Him that He arose and that He is alive and that we are His!

9

Benjamin Franklin's Epitaph

(SUNDAY AFTER EASTER)

JOHN 14:19: ". . . because I live, ye shall live also."

OBJECTS: Two editions of the same book. (I used two editions of *A Dictionary of the Bible* by John D. Davis, Third and Fourth Editions. Another example—I suggest it with modesty—might be my own *A Year of Children's Sermons,* Cokesbury, 1938; Revised Edition, Wilde, 1950.) Also an old book with a badly worn cover.

BENJAMIN FRANKLIN was a very great American. He was one of the founders of our country and his name is one of the greatest names in American history. He began as a printer. And when he came from Boston to Philadelphia to look for work in his trade as a printer, he was very poor. But before he died he became, as you all must know, one of the most important men in the whole country and one of the men who helped get America started as a nation.

When he was 22 years old he wrote an epitaph. An epitaph is a sentence for a gravestone, you know. Now this epitaph that he wrote was for his own grave. But it was never used. I don't know why it was not placed on his grave after his death, for I think it is a wonderful thing, very appropriate, and written by himself for his own grave. But it just was not used. Now this is the way it read:

> The body of B. Franklin, Printer
> (Like the cover of an old Book,
> Its contents torn out
> And stripped of its lettering and gilding)
> Lies here, food for worms.
> But the work shall not be lost,
> For it will (as he believed) appear once more
> In a new and more elegant Edition,
> Revised and corrected
> By the Author.

I used to see this epitaph on a brass plate at the University of Pennsylvania, when I was a student there. That is the school that Benjamin Franklin started. But it was not placed on his grave, even though it was such a lovely sentiment for the tombstone of a printer. But just what did Franklin mean by the words he used on this epitaph?

Well, here are two books that look exactly alike on the outside. They are two editions of the same book. In this case the book is a Bible Dictionary (a very important book, by the way) by John D. Davis. They are two editions of the same book. That is to say, they were made at two different times and printed at two different times. One of these copies is a revised and corrected and changed edition of the other. Some time after the first book was printed, the author felt that he ought to change the book, make corrections in it, bring some of the information in it up to date, perhaps add a little material and altogether make the book more useful, more correct, more perfect, more up to date. So the changes and corrections were all made and the new book printed. This one, then, (hold up later edition) is a revised edition of this one. (Hold up earlier edition.)

Now Franklin said, in his epitaph, that all of us, at death, are like the cover of an old book. Here is an old book. See how the contents are torn out and how the cover is battered, torn, ripped and discolored. Now we are like that at death. The real I and the real you are gone out from the cover. Only the outside remains, torn and battered and ripped and discolored. So when our bodies, after our souls have left them, have been placed in the grave they will be like Franklin's body that he spoke about in these words: "The body of B. Franklin, Printer (Like the cover of an old Book, its contents torn out And stripped of its lettering and gilding) lies here, food for worms."

But some day, at the resurrection, each of us will get a new body. And for each of us, the resurrection body will be new and fine and glorious. That is exactly what Franklin meant in his epitaph when he said: "But the work shall not be lost, For it will (as he believed) appear once more In a new and more elegant Edition, Revised and corrected By the Author." Like an old book that has been revised and corrected and brought up to date, made new and fine and glorious, so the body of each of us will be. It will be like a new book in a new and more elegant edition; and yet, not a new book, either, but the same book, brought out in a new edition, more beautiful and more elegant than before, revised and corrected by the Author. And the Author is God. God made our bodies in the first place. And after our bodies are worn out and discarded and buried in the grave, God will make those same bodies over, renew them, re-make them. God made the first edition of the book which is you and I and Benjamin Franklin. And God will also make the new edition. He is the Author of both.

Now here is the meaning of the resurrection. And here is the meaning of Easter, the great day we celebrated a week ago to-day. Christ rose from the dead. We will rise from the dead. *We are to get a resurrection body.* The body that is buried in the ground will one day, on the resurrection day, be renewed, restored, made glorious, "revised and corrected." It will be a resurrection body.

And here is our text this morning, the text for the boys and girls. Jesus said, ". . . because I live, ye shall live also." You will find this text in God's Book, the Bible, in the Gospel according to John, the 14th chapter and the 19th verse.

There is a lovely old hymn that people used to sing at Easter time and which I think we ought to sing often this time of year. It is a hymn of joy and triumph.

> "Lift your glad voices in triumph on high,
> For Jesus hath risen, and man cannot die."

10

What the Catalog Promises

(SPRING)

1 CORINTHIANS 3:6: "I have planted, Apollos watered; but God gave the increase."

OBJECT: A seed catalog from any nursery or seed company.

I HAVE a spring text for the boys and girls on this spring Sunday. It is from God's Word as we find it written in the First Letter to the Corinthians, the 3rd chapter and the 6th verse: "I have planted, Apollos watered; but God gave the increase."

I have also a spring object for the boys and girls on this spring Sunday. Here is a seed catalog. This booklet tells how to order seeds, roots, bulbs and bushes that you can plant in your gardens in order to grow your own vegetables and flowers. This attractive little book has many pictures in it. Some of them are very large and colored very beautifully. And all of them are placed in the book to show us the vegetables, shrubs and flowers that we can grow from the seeds, roots and bulbs that we buy from the company that sent out the catalog. Here, as we turn over this page, is a beautiful picture of a large, red tomato. And here is a picture of a bunch of lovely sweet peas. Turn a few more pages and we discover a picture of a splendid cluster of juicy, red raspberries. And here is a magnificent dahlia in splendid colors.

Now many people, in early spring, send to different companies for such catalogs. Perhaps some people send to several companies so that they can have several catalogs from several different companies to compare and look over. They love to plan their gardens, often weeks and months ahead of time. They look over their catalogs carefully. They dream of what they will grow. They determine they will plant their seeds and set out their bulbs and put their shrubs and bushes into the ground just as soon as the weather is warm enough and the snow is off and the ground is ready to be worked. They look over the pages of the catalogs very carefully and very often. They get great delight out of studying these pages.

I

Now let us think of the seed catalog a little bit and of the planning people make while they are looking it over. Let us notice what the catalog promises.

1

I have just explained that the catalog contains many pictures, some of them large, all of them attractive, all of them beautiful, of what you are going to grow for yourself, of what you are going to have. That's what makes the catalog interesting. You see in it the things you are going to have some day in your garden. And they are very attractive and very inviting. Here are pictures of what you are going to get.

2

But you must do certain things to get them. You cannot get your vegetables and flowers by dreaming about them, nor by just looking at their pictures in the catalog, nor even by planning, alone. There are certain things you have to do. You have to get the seeds first. And the company that sent you the catalog hopes that you will buy your seeds from them, of course. Then you have to make your ground ready. Then you have to plant the seeds. Then you have to water your garden. You have to cultivate it. You have to hoe it. You have to pull out the weeds. You do all these things, carefully and well, and God makes the plants grow. That is exactly what Paul said in the text I gave you a few minutes ago. He said, you remember, "I have planted, Apollos watered; but God gave the increase."

3

And the result probably will be better than you think! You'll be surprised at the vegetables you get—beans, peas, cabbages, beets. And you'll be delighted at the flowers you produce—pansies, asters, morning-glories, roses. If you do the proper work, if you plant and water and cultivate; you'll get the promised results.

II

Now the Christian life is something like this. What the seed catalog promises makes me think of what the Christian life promises.

1

First of all, we have a picture of what is ahead of us in the Christian life. As the catalog gives a picture of the garden that is promised, so we have a picture of the Christian life that is ahead of us. We get this picture from the Bible and from other Christian people. And the picture of what the Christian life promises is a beautiful picture. It shows us the joy and happiness of serving Jesus, here and now, to-morrow and the day after to-morrow, every day of our lives and as long as we live. The joy and happiness of serving Jesus. And more than that and beyond that, the picture we have shows us the glory and the beauty and the contentment of heaven, where God is and where we some day will be with Him.

2

But we must do certain things to get this picture fulfilled, to have the promise kept. We must believe. We must trust. We must obey. There is an old, old hymn, your fathers and mothers used to sing in Sunday School. I hope some day you will sing it, too. It tells us how important it is to trust and obey. Its chorus says:

> "Trust and obey, for there's no other way
> To be happy in Jesus, but to trust and obey."

So we must believe. We must trust. We must obey. We have to do our part to get the beauties out of the Christian life that are promised. Just as Paul said in our text, "I have planted, Apollos watered; but God gave the increase." We must believe. We must trust. We must obey. And God will give us the life.

3

And the result will be better than you think. You will then live with Jesus all the days of your life. And your life will be one of joy and peace and happiness. And more than that, and beyond that, heaven will be ahead; heaven with all its splendor and all its glory and all its joy.

11

Mother Knows Best

(MOTHER'S DAY)

JOHN 19:25: "Now there stood by the cross of Jesus his mother."

OBJECT: A carnation.

OUR text this morning, boys and girls, on Mother's Day is to be found in God's Book, the Bible, in the Gospel according to John, the 19th chapter and the 25th verse: "Now there stood by the cross of Jesus his mother." And our object for Mother's Day is this carnation, the typical flower for Mother's Day. Each of us wears a carnation, you know, as each of us comes to Church to-day in honor of Mother.

A little while ago, all over our country, High School pupils were asked what they disliked most in their fathers, in their mothers and in themselves. Then they were asked what they liked most in their fathers, in their mothers and in themselves. This same thing was done in summer conferences, too, in all parts of America. We tried it also in our own Young People's Fellowship meeting one night. And what did we discover? About the same thing that was discovered in young people's groups all over the United States.

Now I am going to give you a list of the things that the young folks said all over this country that they disliked most.* In their mothers, the things they said they disliked most were: temper, worrisome, nervousness, nags too much, impatience, too strict, too critical. In their fathers they disliked: temper, stubbornness, too strict, drinks too much, smokes too much, impatience, irritability. And in themselves the traits they most disliked were: temper, selfishness, stubbornness, laziness, quarreling, impatience, shyness.

Now here were the things they liked about fathers, mothers, selves all over the country. Character traits they most admired in their mothers were: understanding, love, kindness, patience, generosity. And in their fathers: good humor, understanding, kindness, friendliness, ability for work. And the traits in themselves they liked best were: friendliness, honesty, personality, understanding, and helpfulness.

Now I told you that our own group of young people, here in our own Church, made the same kind of survey and filled out the same kind of questionnaire. And they came to about the same conclusions. They disliked very much the same things and they liked very much the same things. But in telling about the things they liked, our own group of young folks stressed two things. They liked most of all in their fathers, generosity. And they liked most of all in their mothers, understanding. Most

* Information from "Society Kit," Vol. IV, copyrighted, 1946 by The Westminster Press. All material therefrom used by permission.

of them said that their fathers were generous and they liked that. And most of them said that their mothers were understanding and they liked that.

Now I think that right there is a wonderful thought for Mother's Day. Most of us think that our mothers are understanding. And that is the thing we like best. That is a great thought about Mother, isn't it? That is a great tribute to pay her. (A tribute is a fine compliment, you know.) That is indeed a wonderful thought for Mother's Day. Mother can sympathize. She knows us best. She knows what is best for us. She understands. Mother knows best.

And this is really true. She knows us. She knows what is best for us. Mother understands. Mother knows best.

I think this is where our text fits in. "Now there stood by the cross of Jesus his mother." Jesus Christ was on the cross. And His mother was there, standing by Him. She felt for Him. She understood Him. She knew His suffering. And she stood by Him to the very end. She was there at His side. She loved Him. She felt for Him. She sympathized with Him. She felt His sufferings in her own heart. His dying before her eyes broke her heart. Because she knew Him. She understood Him. She loved Him.

In some such way our mothers know us. Each of us should remember and each of us should realize that Mother knows us. Don't forget that. Remember it always. Mother knows us best because she loves us best.

Mother knows best.

12

"So Busy with Candy, Forgot the Soup."

ECCLESIASTES 3:4: "A time to weep, and a time to laugh; a time to mourn, and a time to dance."

OBJECTS: A candy bar or a bag of candy and a can of soup.

THE other day, toward supper-time, I was in the grocery store. While I was getting my groceries together, a little girl hurried in, ran up to the counter, picked up a package lying on it and ran out, saying, "I was so busy with my candy, I forgot my soup."

Now, what do you suppose she meant by that? I think I know exactly. No doubt her mother had sent her to the store a little while before that to buy a can of soup for the family's supper. She had come into the store and had bought the soup. Probably it came in a can like this. And the can of soup was placed in a bag for her and she had paid for it. Then, probably, she bought some candy. Maybe it looked like this candy I have with me this morning. Anyhow, she bought some candy and paid for that, too. And then, because she was so busy with her candy, she went out of the store without her soup, the very thing she came for. She came on this errand to buy soup for supper. She started for home without the soup she came to buy. She bought it all right. She paid for it and it was wrapped up for her. But she went off without it and it was left lying on the counter. All because, besides the soup, she bought herself some candy, and she was so busy with the candy, she forgot the soup!

Did anything like that ever happen to you? Did you ever get so busy with something you didn't come to do, that you forgot the thing you did come to do?

Now that little saying of the little girl made me think of a verse in the Bible. And I want to share it with you. It will be our children's text this morning. It is found in the Old Testament book of Ecclesiastes, the 3rd chapter and the 4th verse. And this is what it says: "A time to weep, and a time to laugh; a time to mourn, and a time to dance." There is a proper time for most everything. "A time to weep, and a time to laugh; a time to mourn, and a time to dance."

I

There is a time in life for fun. That is what our text is saying and that is what the little girl made me think of. There is a proper time for fun in life. There is a time for joy. There is a time for happiness. There is a good and proper time for sweets. Candy is perfectly right and proper at the right time and in the right place. God wants us to be happy! NEVER FORGET THAT! And also remember that nobody is truly happy without God!

II

But also let us remember that there is a time for serious business. If there is a time for fun, there is also a time for the serious things of life. If God intends us to be happy at the proper time and in the proper place, God also wants us to be serious in the proper place and at the proper time. There is a time for serious business: School, Church, Sunday School, Junior Church, Week Day Religious Education, Making a Living. Life cannot be all fun. Life has also to be serious and there is a time and there is a place for serious business.

Theodore Roosevelt, one of our great Presidents, used to say something like this: "When you play, play hard; when you work, don't play at all." * One of my teachers in school used to quote this over and over because she thought it said so plainly to us that there is a time and a place for all things. "When you play, play hard; when you work, don't play at all." Play when you play; work when you are supposed to work. Don't mix them up and spoil both. There is a time for fun and there is a time for serious business.

III

The third thing our text says to me and the third thing the saying of our little girl makes me think of is just this. We should have a proper time for both play and work. Have a time for your play. It is right and proper. Have also a time for your work. That, too, is right. Don't let one interfere with the other.

IV

And there is a fourth thing to notice. Don't let your play crowd out the more important things. The candy

* The nearest printed saying of Roosevelt to this motto, often repeated by my teacher, that I can discover is as follows: "It is wise to obey the homely old adage, 'Work while you work; play while you play,' " from the essay "The American Boy" found in *The Strenuous Life, Essays and Addresses* by Theodore Roosevelt, published 1901 by the Century Co. I extend cordial thanks to Appleton-Century-Crofts, Inc., owners of the copyright, for permission to quote it here.

is all right, but the soup is more important. Because candy is pleasure mostly, while soup is nourishment and food; and nourishment and food are necessary to health and life. So do not let the candy crowd out the soup. And this applies to lots of other things beside candy and soup. Don't let your play crowd out the more important things.

V

And let God lead you. He wants you to be happy. But He also wants you to be useful. Did you know you are in the world to do His will? To do what He wants? Did you know that? Did you ever stop to think of that? That's what you are here for. To do God's will. To do what God wants done. To do what He intends you to do for Him. Find out what that thing is He wants you to do. And do it.

*   *   *   *

Then you will be happy. Then you will be useful.

13

A Bottle of Milk

(RURAL LIFE SUNDAY)

JUDGES 4:19: "And he said unto her, Give me, I pray thee, a little water to drink; for I am thirsty. And she opened a bottle of milk, and gave him drink, and covered him."

OBJECT: A milk-bottle.

Boys and girls, I have a milk-bottle in my hand. I want to talk about it with you for a little while because to-day is Rural Life Sunday. Did you know that the Bible speaks about a bottle of milk? I wonder how many of you knew that or how many of your parents knew that that very expression, "a bottle of milk," appears in the Bible. Well it does. And to prove it to you, I am going to read for our text this morning the 19th verse of the 4th chapter of the Book of Judges. "And he said unto her, Give me, I pray thee, a little water to drink; for I am thirsty. And she opened a bottle of milk, and gave him drink, and covered him." Now I selected this text because it speaks of a bottle of milk. Of course the bottles used in the time of the Judges were different from the bottles we find on our front porches each morning after the milkman has made his delivery. They used a different kind of bottle altogether in those days from the one we use to-day. Probably it was more like a bag made of skin from a lamb or a goat. But the Bible calls it a bottle and it held milk.

I

Now when you think of a bottle of milk, you think of many things, I am sure. One of the things I think of is the fact that the cream on the milk rises to the top. You have noticed that, I am sure. Maybe you have even seen your mother pour the cream off the top of the bottle to have cream for her coffee before she shakes the bottle or stirs it up and pours out a gleaming glassful for you to drink. The cream is the best part of the milk. It is the most expensive. If you bought just cream, a bottle of it would cost many times what an equal bottle of milk would cost. The cream is the richest part, the best part, the most expensive part. And it rises to the top.

Now that is exactly the way it is in life. The best gets to the top. At least it is usually that way. The best player on the team gets the top place. The best student goes to the head of the class. The best worker gets the best job. So it is a good idea, isn't it, for us to study hard, to work diligently, to pray fervently to get to the top. Let us ask God's help. Let us try to get ahead.

II

There is a second thing this bottle of milk says to me. It is just that milk, according to the best of doctors and the best of health authorities, is the perfect food. The other day on a trip to Ogdensburg, I saw two huge signs, erected by the State of New York I think, between Gouverneur and the city of Ogdensburg. Both of them said: "DRINK MORE MILK."

Nature provides it. Man does not manufacture it. Man does not combine several different products to make it. Man does not have to doctor it up. Nature produces it exactly as we drink it; *all complete, all made.* And it has in it, when we get it to drink, everything that we need for life. Who could plan and prepare it? Surely, no one less than God. Surely it makes us think of Him, when we stop to figure that it is the perfect food all made up and put together and ready for us to use. God gives it.

All good gifts come from God.

III

But there is one more thing this bottle is saying to me. If it reminds me that milk is the perfect food, it is also reminding me that there are in the world to-day some other drinks that are not good, but are bad. Milk is good. Some drinks are bad. You know which ones I mean. You know the names of the bad ones. I certainly hope you do not know the taste of them! If it is a good rule to say, "Drink more milk"; there is also another good rule which says, "Never drink alcohol." For alcohol is a poison. Milk is a good drink. Anything with alcohol in it is a bad drink. It is just as simple as that. It is just as easy to figure out as that. It is just as plain as that.

The other day I saw a motion picture which was called, "They Were Expendable." It was about the Second World War and the Philippines. In one place in the picture some service men in the great city of Manila were drinking a toast to the United States Navy. One boy drank the toast in milk. (The rest were drinking beer and wine.) He was very anxious to praise the United States Navy and wish it success, just as the others wanted to do. But he would not drink what the other soldiers were drinking. He insisted on drinking milk and he got his milk to drink. He had the best drink of all! He was the best boy of all!

14

"What Mean Ye by This Service?"

(MEMORIAL DAY)

❧❧

EXODUS 12:26: ". . . your children shall say unto you, What mean ye by this service?"

OBJECT: An American Flag.

❧❧

IN GOD's Book, the Bible, there is a text that I want to read to the boys and girls this morning. It is found in the Book of Exodus (the second book in the Bible, you boys and girls know), the 12th chapter and the 26th verse. And in that verse we read: ". . . your children shall say unto you, What mean ye by this service?"

This text was spoken by Moses when he was explaining to the Children of Israel the meaning of the Passover. And he told them that in the years to come their children would ask what the Passover meant and why the Jewish people were having a celebration. Many, many years after the first Passover took place, the Jewish people would still be celebrating that great event. And the children in each family would ask to be told what the celebration was for. And the father of the family would tell them what it meant. "What mean ye by this service?" the children would ask. And then the father of the house would tell them the meaning.

Now what Moses predicted has come to pass. For the Jews all over the world once a year still celebrate the

Passover feast. And it has become a part of the ritual of that celebration to have this question asked and answered. I mean, it is a regular part of the celebration at Passover time and it is still used to-day. The youngest person present asks this question of the father of the family, "What mean ye by this service?" and then the father explains.

The Passover feast to-day, as you know, is the Jewish feast so much thought of by modern Jews, celebrated about the time we Christians celebrate Easter. The purpose of the feast is to remind all the Jewish people of the wonderful occasion when the Angel of Death came to Egypt and killed the eldest child in every Egyptian family but "passed over" the Jewish homes and left the oldest child in each Jewish house unharmed. The oldest child in every Egyptian home was dead. The Israelites were spared. And because of that great event, the people of Israel were saved. And so the Passover is also a great celebration of the deliverance of the Children of Israel from Egypt and slavery.

This week we are to have a celebration in America. Everywhere we shall see flags flying. It will be a wonderful occasion. It will be a very special day. Everywhere throughout this vast and glorious land there will be special services to observe this very special day. And I am sure that there will be children everywhere who will be asking a question very like the one we are talking about. It will be Memorial Day, and I am sure that many a child, as he sees the parade and beholds the soldiers and hears the addresses and listens to the firing of the volley over the grave of a soldier will ask the question, "What mean ye by this service?"

What do we mean by Memorial Day? Why Memorial

Day, as its name shows, is a day to remember. On it we remember our heroes, especially our soldiers and sailors, those men and women who served our great country during all the wars of our history. Memorial Day, of course, began as a day of remembrance for the soldiers of the great Civil War in our country, many years ago. But we now use it as a special day on which to remember the heroes of all wars. And I think that Memorial Day means more each year to the American people because we realize that as the years come and go more and more persons have given their lives in American wars to keep our country and to keep alive the great hopes and ideals of America and to promote peace all over the world. Memorial Day means much to us in these days, for the great and terrible Second World War has not been over very long and all of us know of people in our own families or among our friends who were wounded or even killed in that dreadful war. One of our own Church members died at Pearl Harbor, when World War II began as far as America was concerned. Silas A. Wainwright was in the Navy and he was on the famous U.S.S. Arizona which was sunk at Pearl Harbor the very day the war started. And after him several other members of our own Church gave their lives for their country before the war was over and many others were wounded and many, many more were in the fight. And since that time, soldiers and sailors from around here have gone to Korea to uphold the honor of our country and to help bring peace once more to the world.

So on Memorial Day we remember all those who fought for God and country. Memorial Day makes us think of all who gave us our country and our freedom.

Once there was a famous man named Cato. He was a Roman. He lived many, many years ago in ancient Rome and he was a great statesman and patriot, that is, he served his country and loved it very much. According to Plutarch, a famous writer who told us much about great men, Cato once said: "I had rather men should ask why my statue is not set up, than why it is." * Do you see what Cato meant? He would much rather have people wonder why no statue of him was set up than why one was. He would rather serve his country and not have any glory and recognition for it than not serve his country and have people praise him and erect monuments to him. So we say sometimes, "Why don't we have monuments for all the men who saved our country in the days of danger and war and for those who are called upon to go out to distant places and fight for our beloved country now?" Well, we just cannot have monuments for all of them. We cannot have a great monument for every soldier and every sailor who fought and died for America. There have been so many brave men and women who did this for us that we just would not have room for all the monuments. But they deserve it. So Memorial Day has to be sort of a monument. Memorial Day must be thought of as a monument to them all. Ah! There we have it! That is what the day is for. That is what we mean by the service of Memorial Day. The very Day itself is a monument to them all.

* Plutarch 46 (?)-120 (?) A.D. *Political Precepts.*

15

The Piano

❧❧

2 Chronicles 7:6: ". . . instruments of music. . . ."

Object: The piano in Church or Sunday School.

❧❧

Boys and girls, you remember that a little while ago I asked you to tell me some of the things you would like me to make Children's Sermons about; to draw lessons from. Some of you asked me to speak about the strangest things: a frying-pan, a snowball, an electric light bulb, a board in a house, the moon, stars, ice-cream, candy, a piano. This morning, then, I am going to make the Children's Sermon about "The Piano." The object for you to look at is the piano here in Church. It is too heavy and too large for me to bring into the pulpit, as I usually do with the objects that I use for the talks to the boys and girls. But I think you will pardon me for this.

Well, the piano is the object this morning. And here is the text: 2 Chronicles 7:6, just part of the verse, where it says, ". . . instruments of music. . . ."

The Bible speaks many times of instruments of music. And it mentions many different kinds of instruments. It speaks of the bell, of the trumpet, and of the cymbal. It mentions the flute and the harp and the organ. It speaks of the timbrel or tambourine; and many others. But it does not mention the piano. For the piano is a new instrument since Bible days. But let us think of the piano this morning. And you may look at it as I speak if you would like.

I

Now if I asked any one of you what you would say first of all about the piano, I am quite sure that you would say that it makes, or at least can make, beautiful music. That is certainly the first thing any one of us would think about the piano. It makes beautiful music. Well, it certainly does. But I want to tell you that life ought to be like that, too. Life ought to be pleasant, beautiful, full of melody. That's what God wants.

II

Now the second interesting thing about the piano is that many can play it. The piano is not an instrument that only one or two people in a whole town can play. Many people in this town can play the piano. Many people in this Church can play the piano. Many of you boys and girls can play the piano. That is one very fine thing about it. A great many people can play. If you know a little about the piano—only had two or three lessons—you can make pretty music. If you know a lot about it—had many, many lessons—you can make pretty music. Pretty music—maybe not exactly the same music, but pretty music anyhow—can be made by those who know little and those who know a lot. Now that's the way it ought to be with life, too. All kinds of people ought to enjoy life: ignorant and smart people; rich and poor people; important and non-important people; high and low people. All should enjoy life. All should be happy. All people, all kinds of people, all people everywhere.

For God wants all kinds of people to be happy. Happiness and contentment God does not intend just for certain kinds of people, maybe the rich or maybe the very smart. God wants all kinds of people to be happy.

III

Now there is a third thing to notice about the piano. It can be abused. There are several ways in which the piano can be abused. I shall mention only two. For example, there is the discord. A chord is a combination of two or more notes that are struck together that harmonize, that is, that go together, that sound pleasant. A discord is caused by striking notes at the same time that do not harmonize, that is, do not go together, do not sound pleasant and so clash. You can abuse the piano, you see, you can spoil its good music, by discords.

And another way the piano can be abused is by pounding. Some children who cannot play the piano just pound it. I remember my mother scolding me when I was a little boy for pounding on the piano. That abuses the instrument. That spoils the music.

Now life is like that, too. What ought to be beautiful music in your life and mine, can be ruined by using life wrongly. Your life ought to be beautiful music. You can spoil that beautiful music by using your life in the wrong way, in the way it is not intended to be used.

IV

Fourth and last, the piano needs to be kept in tune. You cannot get really good music out of the piano if it is out of tune. And just so it is with life. We must be kept in tune with God to live a happy, harmonious, beautiful life. How can we keep in tune with God?

Through the Church; in the Sunday School; by Bible
study; by prayer.

16

The Shiny Door-Knob *

(CHILDREN'S DAY)

DANIEL 10:6: ". . . polished brass. . . ."

OBJECT: A metal door-knob that can be brought into the pulpit;
or the inside pair of door-knobs on the main doors of the
Church (if these are double doors) or knobs on any double
doors in or near the Church to which attention can be
called.

To-DAY is Children's Day in our Church; one of the
nicest days in the whole year. And on Children's
Day it is my privilege to give a little talk to both the
Church and the Sunday School at the same time. And
that is also a pleasure!

The Bible speaks of polished brass. And I want that
to be our text for the Children's Sermon this Children's
Day. In Daniel 10:6 the Bible speaks of polished brass.

*   *   *   *

Did you ever notice the two door-knobs on our
Church's main front doors? If you never did, I suggest

---

* The object used and the topic of this sermon were suggested to me
by Mrs. Sterling L. Tait, a member of my church. I extend to her hearty
thanks.

that you look at them carefully on your way out of the
Church to-day. One of our members showed them to
me last Sunday! One is shiny and bright. The other is
dull, black and dark. One is like the text, like "polished
brass." The other one is dull and dingy and dark. Why?
Because one is used, is constantly handled, is touched
over and over again and so is kept polished and shiny
from constant handling, touching and rubbing. That
one of course is on the door of the two doors that is
always used; for you must have noticed that ordinarily
when people come in or out of our Church, they almost
always use just one of the two big, main, front doors, the
one that is on your right, coming in. That means, then,
that the knob on the other door, being almost never
used, almost never touched, almost never handled and
therefore almost never rubbed by the hands of the people coming in or going out, is dull and dingy and dark.
Notice that when you leave to-day!

But what are these two door-knobs saying to us to-
day; knobs exactly alike; yet knobs that look so different; one so shiny; one so dull; one that is used and so
polished and shiny; one that is never used and so dingy
and dull? I think they are saying several things to us,
especially five things.

I

First they are saying, "Use Your Talents." What is a
talent? Why, something that you can do well. So, use
your talents. Keep them bright and useful by using
them. The more you use them, the brighter they will be!

II

Secondly, the door-knobs are saying, "Use Your
Smile." It will do good, that smile of yours, if you use

it. It will spoil if you do not. If you do not use your smile, pretty soon you will not have any to use. It is one of those things that must be used to be kept. It is one of those things that you will forget how to use if you do not use it. It is one of those things that you will not be able to make if you stop making it. Use it or lose it!

III

The third thing the door-knobs are saying is, "Use Your Conscience." Your conscience, you know, is God's voice speaking inside you—telling you to do right and telling you not to do wrong. Use it.

I once knew a man who said his conscience was as good as knew, for he never used it! Of course that is not so; that cannot be so! There are a few things in this world that can be kept as good as new by not using them. But conscience is certainly not one of them. You cannot keep it good as new by not using it. If you do not use it, it becomes tarnished and useless. The only way to keep it alive, the only way to keep it new and up to date is to use it. Use your conscience and keep it bright!

IV

Again the door-knobs are saying to each of us, "Use Your Bible." That's what it is for. Don't let dust collect on it. Use it. Read it. Study it! Here is a true story for you. Once a minister was visiting in another town, where he was to preach one Sunday for the regular minister of that Church who was away. The visiting minister was staying on Saturday night in the home of one of the families of that Church. He asked if they had a hymn-book in that house for he would like to see it and pick out his hymns for the service next morning. He was told they had one and the son in the family was asked to bring it to him. The boy went to the music-cabinet and brought out a hymn-book, carried it to the visiting minister, blowing the dust off it as he did so. Seeing this, the visiting minister said, "I'm glad that is not the Bible, from which you are blowing the dust."

Do you see what he meant? He was glad the Bible was used in that home and was not tucked away some place gathering dust. Use your Bible.

V

And the door-knobs also say, "Use Your Religion." That's what God gave it to you for. Use your religion. Keep it bright. Use it.

17

"Ask Your Daddy"

(FATHER'S DAY)

MATTHEW 7:11: "If ye then, being evil, know how to give good gifts unto your children, how much more shall your Father which is in heaven give good things to them that ask him?"

OBJECTS: A toy balloon, a bag of pop-corn, a large piece of taffy or a lollipop, a toy cane, a comical hat, or any other object or objects that will suggest the objects usually bought at a street or country fair.

I HAVE a true story for the boys and girls this morning. I like stories and you like stories, I know. But somehow, I think I like them best when they are true. This is a true story for I heard it with my own ears!

Last summer my family and I crossed the St. Lawrence River on the ferry from Brockville, Ontario, to Morristown, New York on one occasion in the early evening. Maybe all of you remember that ferry that crosses the river at that point. You drive your automobile right onto the deck of the boat, you know, and the boat carries you across the river and you drive off! But while the boat that is carrying your car is crossing the river, most of the people like to get out of the cars on board and stand around watching the progress of the voyage, enjoying the beautiful scenery on the beautiful river at this end of the Thousand Islands, and visiting with each other as the crossing is being made. On this particular night, the lights of the city of Brockville were shining brightly and made a lovely picture as they were reflected in the water. By the brightly colored lights that we could see back in the city we were leaving, it looked as if some sort of fair was going on in Brockville. We could see the colors of the lights. We could see many of them gathered together in one place. We could even see the lights that outlined the great Ferris Wheel as it moved slowly above the crowd.

Now there was a small child on the ferry, standing near us and talking to her mother. I could not help hearing what she was saying. Looking up into her mother's eyes, she asked:

"May I go to the fair?" She must have been looking at the many bright lights. And maybe she was thinking of the things that children like to do at the fair, the things they like to see and the things they like to buy and the things they like to eat. Maybe she was thinking of balloons like this, or pop-corn like this or taffy like this or a cane like this or a funny hat like this. Anyhow, she said, "May I go to the fair?"

And then she went on, "May I ride on the Ferris Wheel?"

And her mother said to her, "Ask your daddy!"

Did you ever hear that said to you? "Ask your daddy." I have heard it many times and I think this little girl had heard it before, too. Now that reply meant two things to me and I think it ought to mean two things to you. Doesn't it mean to you that your father is good to you? And doesn't it also mean that your father knows what is best for you? Surely it means both those things for both those things are true. Your father is good to you. I know he is. And your father always knows what is best for you. You know that, too.

But this is also true of God, your Heavenly Father. Surely God, your Heavenly Father is good to you. And surely God, your Heavenly Father, knows what is best. Indeed it is even MORE true of your Father in heaven than it is of your father on earth. It is true in a higher, finer, better sense. Your human father is good to you; your Heavenly Father is better. Your human father knows what is best; your Heavenly Father knows even better what is best. Jesus told us that one time and His words are going to be our text this morning. Matthew

7:11: "If ye then, being evil, know how to give good gifts unto your children, how much more shall your Father which is in heaven give good things to them that ask him?" If human fathers know how to give good things to their children, how much more does our Father in heaven know how to give good gifts to His children? God gives us good things. God gives us what we need. God knows what is best. For Jesus said in another place, ". . . your heavenly Father knoweth that ye have need of all these things." *

And then Jesus added still another thought, in still another place (this is in Luke 11:13 while our text was from Matthew 7:11): "If ye then, being evil, know how to give good gifts unto your children: how much more shall your heavenly Father give the Holy Spirit to them that ask him?" In Matthew Jesus said that God would give His children good things; and in Luke He adds that one of the good things that God will give His children is the Holy Spirit. God will give us the Holy Spirit. That means that God will give us Himself, for the Holy Spirit is God as the Father is God and as the Son is God. So when God gives us the Holy Spirit He gives us Himself. He comes into us. He helps us believe. He helps us pray. He helps us live.

He does this if we ask Him; if we have faith. So, boys and girls, we must have faith. Let us have faith. Let us believe. Let us ask. Let us ask God. ASK YOUR HEAVENLY FATHER!

* Matthew 6:32

18

"Oh Say, Can You See?"

(FLAG DAY)

Isaiah 13:2: "Lift ye up a banner. . . ."

Object: An American flag.

FLAG DAY comes this week. And to-day, the Sunday before Flag Day, I have a Flag Day text. It is found in the Old Testament, in the ancient prophecy of Isaiah, in the 13th chapter and at the 2nd verse: "Lift ye up a banner. . . ." Is that not what we do with the Star-Spangled Banner? When we fly Old Glory to the breeze, do we not lift up a banner? I hold in my hand an American flag. We are proud of it. And well we may be. For our flag is a great flag and our flag has had a great history.

On June 14, 1777, Congress passed a law saying that the flag of our beloved country, America, was to consist of thirteen stripes and thirteen stars. Later two new states came into the union and so two stripes were added to the flag and two stars. So once the American flag had fifteen stripes and fifteen stars.

Now this was the flag that Francis Scott Key saw when he wrote our national anthem, "The Star-Spangled Banner." At this time England and the United States were at war. It is called The War of 1812. The

British burned our capital city, Washington, in 1814. Then they attacked the great city of Baltimore. Mr. Key was a lawyer who lived in the city of Washington. He had gone to Baltimore on business under a flag of truce. But the enemy captured him just the same and he was held a captive on a British war-ship and was on that ship, a prisoner, while the British fleet bombarded the city of Baltimore and the famous fort, called Fort McHenry, which was the city's defense.

All night long, September 13, 1814, the British ships bombarded the fort. Key watched the fight from the deck of the ship which was his prison. He paced back and forth acrss the deck, wondering all night through if the flag which he saw there on the fort at nightfall would still be there by morning. So all night he watched, trying by the flash of the guns and the explosions all about him to catch a glimpse of the flag he loved. The flash of fire that spit out every now and then, and

". . . the rockets' red glare, the bombs bursting in air,
Gave proof through the night that our flag was still there!"

Morning came. He looked through the "mists of the deep," in "the dawn's early light," straining to see.

The flag was still there! The fort had not surrendered. Old Glory was still waving in the breeze, which

"As it fitfully blows, half conceals, half discloses."

Then, in patriotic joy and thanksgiving, he composed "The Star-Spangled Banner." He wrote it on the back of an envelope he found in his pocket, while he was still standing on the deck of the British battle-ship and further as he rode in a little rowboat which took him to shore.

Now this is a wonderful song, our National Anthem, and there are many things that it teaches us, especially the great third stanza.

I

"............................freemen shall stand
  Between their loved homes and the war's desolation."

Here the song is saying that true and free men will defend their homes!

II

"Blest with vict'ry and peace, may the heaven-rescued land
  Praise the Power that hath made and preserved us a nation!"

God made and God preserved us a nation. We owe our start and our preservation to God. Let us praise Him!

III

"Then conquer we must, when our cause it is just,
  And this be our motto: 'IN GOD IS OUR TRUST!' "

We will win if our cause is *right*. All our hope ought to be, "In God is our Trust."

IV

Then we can sing:

"And the star-spangled banner in triumph shall wave
  O'er the land of the free and the home of the brave!"

Trust God, do right. Then our land will be filled with people who are brave and who are free. Trust God, do right. Then America will be the land of the free and of the brave!

What better ideas can we have on Flag Day?
Let us defend our beloved homes.
Let us thank God for America.
Let us always and ever stand for the right.
Let us put our trust in God!
Then our land will be safe. Then America will be

". . . the land of the free and the home of the brave!"

19

Ice-Cream

(SUMMER)

JOB 38:22: "Hast thou entered into the treasures of the snow? or hast thou seen the treasures of the hail?"

PSALM 147:16-17: "He giveth snow like wool: he scattereth the hoarfrost like ashes. He casteth forth his ice like morsels: who can stand before his cold?"

OBJECT: A cardboard container, such as ice-cream is sold in in local stores.

WE ARE going to talk about ice-cream in our children's sermon this morning. This topic was suggested by one of the congregation. We often take topics that the boys and girls suggest themselves, you know. And this morning it is ice-cream. Here is a cardboard container such as you find in stores which sell ice-cream.

It is our object to make you think of the thing I am going to talk about.

I like ice-cream. So I am glad to talk about it. Ice-cream is not mentioned in the Bible. It had not yet been invented in Bible times. But ice and snow are mentioned in the Bible many times. For example, in Job. 38:22 we read, "Hast thou entered into the treasures of the snow? or hast thou seen the treasures of the hail?" And in the 147th Psalm, in the 16th and 17th verses we read, "He giveth snow like wool: he scattereth the hoarfrost like ashes. He casteth forth his ice like morsels: who can stand before his cold?" The Bible knew ice and snow and hail and frost. But the Bible knows nothing of ice-cream. We know ice and snow and hail and frost. And we know ice-cream, too. Let's talk about ice-cream for a moment.

I

First of all, let us notice that ice-cream is good for you. Isn't it fine that ice-cream, something that is good, is good for us? You know some things that you like are good for you. And some things you like are not. Too much candy, say, and too much ice-cream are not good for us. Eating between meals. Skipping school. Skipping Sunday School. Telling a lie. Cheating. Some of these things we may like, or we may think we like, but they are not good for us. Ice-cream, in the right place and at the right time, is.

II

The second thing I notice about ice-cream is that you must eat it when it is ready. It will keep a good long time in the refrigerator or in the cooler or in the deep freeze. But once it is served, we must eat it or it will melt and will be no good.

But just so there are a great many things that we must do at the right time. If we do them at all, if we expect any good to come out of them, if we expect to accomplish anything, there are some things that we must do just at the right time. For example, giving to missions should be done when the gift is needed. It will not do much good when it is not needed. And when it is needed it is sometimes needed very much! We should attend Sunday School and Church at the right time. It would be silly to attend Church when there was no service in session. It would be silly to attend Sunday School when there was no Sunday School. Many things in life have to be done at the right time or it is not much use doing them.

III

There is a third thing that I have noticed about ice-cream. It will spoil if we put it in the wrong place. Don't put your ice-cream on the kitchen stove. That's the wrong place. It will spoil if you put it there. Don't put it on the hot air register or the steam radiator. Don't put it in the washing machine.

But did you know that we, too, will spoil if we are in the wrong place? We will spoil if we are in the place we ought not be, the place we do not belong. The saloon is one such place. That will spoil any one of us and spoil us in a hurry! The cheap dance hall is another such place. The street is still another such place if we are found there instead of being in Church and Sunday School at Church and Sunday School time, where we belong!

IV

One more thing about ice-cream. It will spoil if we forget it. Once there was an ice-cream cone put on the hall table. A little girl who had bought it, brought it home and started to eat it, placed it there in a very great hurry when she ran up-stairs to see a new dress that had come for her that day. And because she was so excited about the new dress, she forgot all about her ice-cream. It was spoiled when she returned!

Our Christian life is something like that. It will spoil unless we tend to it. If we forget it, this Christian life of ours; if we run off and leave it; if we do not pay any attention to it; it will spoil. The same thing is true of our Christian deeds. If we pay no attention to them; if we neglect them; if we expect they will take care of themselves; if we run off and leave them; if we do not keep our eyes on them; they will spoil, melt away, disappear.

Don't neglect your Christian faith. Keep it alive. Keep it fresh. Keep it working.

Don't neglect your Christian life. Keep it wide-awake and vigorous and active.

Don't neglect your Christian duty. Don't let it spoil because you do not practice it. Keep it new. Keep it shiny. Keep it alive.

20

The Big Noise

(INDEPENDENCE DAY)

❧

LEVITICUS 25:10: ". . . proclaim liberty throughout all the land unto all the inhabitants thereof. . . ."

OBJECT: A large firecracker, either real or imitation.

❧

OUR text to-day is found in God's Word, in the Book of Leviticus, in the 25th chapter and at the 10th verse: ". . . proclaim liberty throughout all the land unto all the inhabitants thereof. . . ." That's our text. And here's our object, this giant firecracker. Both are for Independence Day, which, as you all know, comes on July 4th.

Now Americans used to use firecrackers on Independence Day, July 4th, always. It just wasn't the Fourth of July unless there were explosions all over the place. Firecrackers going off here; torpedoes that would explode with a great bang when hurled down upon the sidewalk, making their noise there; cap-pistols being shot in that direction; toy cannons being shot in this. Here was noise; there was noise; everywhere was noise, as people celebrated Independence Day. When I was a boy, we all had firecrackers to explode and the popping and the banging of the explosions could be heard all around us, all day long.

And then at night we would have fancy fireworks—

sky-rockets that would shoot up into the heavens and explode with a wonderful display of sparks and brilliantly colored balls; Roman candles that would be held in the hand and, once lighted, would shoot out a shower of sparks out of which would come brightly colored balls at regular intervals; pin-wheels that spun and glowed and shot out fire; mystic flower-pots and fire-fountains and burning balls and buzzing volcanoes and flaming designs and glowing stars. What a wonderful night it was with all the fireworks and all the family and all the friends gathered around to see the grand display. Why I can remember, when I was a boy at home, that some years my father would spend five dollars on firecrackers and other noise makers for the afternoon and fireworks for the grand display at night. And some years he would go up as high as six dollars. And once I think he spent nine. But then we had a big family, and there were always guests invited to come and sit on the lawn and watch the fireworks in the early evening. And the noise of the day always continued into the night. It was a day to celebrate. It was a day to shoot off the firecrackers. It was the day of the Big Noise.

I

But Independence Day is not just noise. I suppose when this country was first free the people were so very glad that they made a lot of noise about it. They shot off cannons and they shot off guns and they made a loud and a lusty celebration. I suppose that is exactly how the custom got started to have a lot of noise on the Fourth of July. Fortunately, the law in most states to-day does not allow us to shoot off firecrackers as we used to do. It got to be really very dangerous, you know. But after all,

Independence Day should mean more to us than just noise. We should get at the meaning of the day. We should try to understand what liberty is and how much it is worth.

II

And true independence is not just a big noise one day and then all forgotten. Liberty is a very important thing. We are very proud of our independence and our liberty in this country. It is not just noise. It is something that we fought to get and that we fought to keep. And it is something that we should cherish and protect.

III

The noise on Independence Day is really to show that we are glad and thankful. But let us remember what we are glad and thankful about—our country, our liberty, our independence. We should not make noise just for the sake of noise. The fun and celebration and the noise of the Fourth of July is all to show we are thankful and glad we are Americans, that we have a great and a free country, that we rule ourselves, that liberty and justice and equality are all ours. So let us remember that in all our celebrating and in all our noise making. Let us remember what we are glad and thankful about.

But more important still, let us remember that God has given our country all that makes it great and good and strong. Without His help, we never would have had our independence. Without God's direction, we never would have become free. Without God's kindness to us, we never could have won our liberty. Without God's goodness, we never would have our beloved country, and all its resources and all its wealth and all its greatness. Let us remember God. Let us remember that God made America.

21

*Road-Signs**

(SUMMER)

ISAIAH 30:21: "And thine ears shall hear a word behind thee, saying, This is the way, walk ye in it, when ye turn to the right hand, and when ye turn to the left."

OBJECT: An imitation road-sign made out of bristol-board and lettered by black crayon; e.g. "CROSS × ROAD."

I THINK I did a very smart thing when I asked the boys and girls to tell me some things that they would like me to make talks to boys and girls about. The Children's Sermon this morning was suggested to me by an older boy in our congregation. He asked me to talk sometime about "Road-Signs." You know we see many road-signs as we go along the highways in our cars. They tell us what is ahead of us. They explain to the drivers what the road is like. They give warning as to what to expect ahead. They help us to be careful. And thus they help us to drive.

One sign may read, "DANGEROUS CURVE." Another, "STOP—THRU TRAFFIC." Here we may see, "CROSS ROAD"; and there, "STEEP HILL." Another

---

* This sermon was suggested by Mr. William B. Simons, a member of the Gouverneur Church, to whom I give hearty thanks.

sign might say, "ONE WAY," and another, "DEAD
END STREET." "NARROW BRIDGE," one would
tell us. "KEEP TO RIGHT," another would say.

So the signs help us. They tell us how to go, where to
be careful, what to look out for, where to turn, where
to stop, how to avoid accident and trouble.

But so it is in life. God will do all this for us. Just as
the State and County Highway Departments help us
drive along the road, so God will help us move along
the highway of life. He will help us, He will tell us how
to go, where to be careful, what to look out for, where to
turn, where to stop, how to avoid accident and trouble.
The Bible tells us that God will do all this for us. That is
why I have a text this morning. You will find it in
Isaiah 30:21 where you will read, "And thine ears shall
hear a word behind thee, saying, This is the way, walk
ye in it, when ye turn to the right hand, and when ye
turn to the left." Does not that sound exactly like a road-
sign for the highway of life? "This is the way, walk ye
in it, when ye turn to the right hand, and when ye turn
to the left." God gives us road-signs all through our
lives to help us on our way.

One way He does this is through our parents. Their
instructions to us are like road-signs on the path of life.
They point to dangers and show us the way. We may
heed these signs our parents give us or not. We may follow the advice they give or let it pass by. We may obey
the signs they give us or refuse to obey. This is up to us.
But at least they have warned us!

I

Here is a sign our parents might give us, "DANGER-
OUS CURVE." As on the highway, so in life, there are

times when such a sign would tell us we ought to go slowly. Many things in life are like dangerous curves and the signs our parents and others have put up for us would tell us to go slowly, very slowly. For instance a dance with liquor up at Sylvia Lake. "Go slow," is certainly the advice at such a place. If you go anywhere near it, watch out!

II

"STOP STREET," another sign says, both for the highway and for life. There are times when we ought to stop. Going into a saloon is one. The word is "STOP."

III

"CROSS ROAD," is another sign. On the highway and in life that means that somebody else may be coming along and your paths may meet. That other person has rights, too. Don't interfere with them or you will get into trouble. Think of the other fellow. That's what the "CROSS ROAD" sign means for life.

IV

"STEEP HILL," will be a sign at the bottom of a steep up-grade. That means, in life as on the road, use all your power; there is a hard job ahead. There are times when you need all your *strength* or *courage*.

V

Or the "STEEP HILL" sign may mean that the road is about to go down. There are many places in life where you have to use your brakes. Certain things are proper and right if you don't go too far or too fast. Watch. Be careful. Go slow.

VI

"ONE WAY," is another sign. Some streets and some roads can be traveled in only one direction. Some things we do in life we can never undo. Some mean remark you just can't unsay! Some mean act you may do some time and it will hurt others, and once you get started on it perhaps you cannot stop. Many things you can't undo or unsay. So be sure you are right before you go ahead.

VII

Here is another sign, "DEAD END STREET." Now that means that this street, if you are talking about highways, or that thing that you are starting out to do, if you are talking about life, will take you only so far and no farther. So watch and be careful. Are you sure you want to go on this street or start out to do this thing? Maybe it is some job you want. Maybe some deed you want to do. Is it going to be a dead end street? Know where it leads you. Know what you want. Know if you really want to do it. Know if it is right.

VIII

And then we come to a sign that reads, "NARROW BRIDGE." That tells us to be very careful as we go along. Walk the straight and narrow path. Don't start out on a narrow bridge if another is coming toward you and is ready to run into you. A collision and all kinds of trouble may result. Also, don't swerve to one side or the other when you are on a narrow bridge. Keep straight! That's good advice for the highway and for life. Keep straight!

IX

"KEEP TO RIGHT," is a sign we often see. Do the right thing, ALWAYS. "KEEP TO THE RIGHT." That's a good rule on the highway. That's a good rule all through life!

22

"Thanks, I Don't Drink."

OBJECT: A toy airplane.

"THANKS, I don't drink; just give me a glass of water." These words have become famous and they are worthy of a high place in our memories. They do credit to a very fine and a very famous young man, about whom I am going to tell you in a moment.

"Thanks, I don't drink; just give me a glass of water." These were almost the first words that Douglas Corrigan, the 31 year old "flying mechanic" who startled the world by hopping over the Atlantic Ocean to Ireland in his antique $900 "aerial jalopy" a few years ago, spoke after he landed in that foreign land. And one of the very first pictures that was radioed to the United States after his wonderful feat showed him drinking water after he had refused a glass of Irish whiskey. For Douglas Corrigan announced to all the world after that famous flight that he neither drank nor smoked.

At the time when his name was in all the papers for the daring deed that he performed in the worn-out airplane, he lived with his uncle, who was the pastor of a Baptist Church in Santa Monica, California. He said at the time, "Water is good enough for me. Liquor and flying do not mix." His aim was to lead a clean life. He was a member of a Protestant Church. And his life's ambition was to be a good flyer. And he made it perfectly clear to every one that to be a good flyer, one needed a clear head.

His famous flight will help teach youth the value of clean living and total abstinence. And he will always be remembered as one who did a daring deed with a clear head and who would not drink intoxicating beverages either before or after the flight. How true his words were and how much we ought to listen to them. Liquor and flying do not mix. One who drinks alcoholic beverages ought not to try to fly. One who wants to fly certainly ought not to drink drinks with alcohol in them. For liquor and flying do not mix.

Douglas Corrigan (it was several years ago, now) took off from Floyd Bennett Field in New York on a certain day. He was just a young mechanic who owned and cherished a tumbled-down airplane. Nobody paid much attention to him. He was not very well known. But in a day he became famous.

Everybody thought that he was going to California that particular day when he climbed into his air jalopy and rose into the air. And his arrival in Dublin, Ireland, a few hours later, was the first idea any one had that he was not on his way to the West Coast. He was soon called "Wrong Way Corrigan." For he set out, every one supposed, for California. And he landed in Ireland!

Still in his greasy flying togs, after his famous flight, he met Eamon De Valera, the famous Irish Premier, who welcomed him to Ireland most cordially, praised him for his record flight, and said, "As long as you choose to stay in this country, you shall be an honored guest of Ireland."

Corrigan was more proud of his ship than of his great achievement. "She's in grand condition, after that hop," he said. "I think she could take me around the world."

Corrigan did a brave thing, a wonderful thing, an unexpected thing. How the world was surprised when it discovered that this young man who had set out for California from New York City a few hours before had arrived in Ireland! "Wrong Way Corrigan" became famous at once. Indeed his flight, unknown to anybody, with no one to help him, with no one to guard him, with no one to follow him across the mighty ocean, with no one to look for him if his poor, old plane should meet with difficulty and be forced down onto the water, was a most remarkable thing. He deserved to become famous. He deserved to have the whole world acclaim him a hero.

But the most remarkable thing about the whole flight, it seems to me, is that simple and noble sentence that he uttered when he was offered a drink. That sentence would be a good motto for us. That sentence could very well become the rule of our lives. That sentence will keep us out of lots of trouble and away from all kinds of sorrow. Let us adopt it as our motto. Let us make it the rule of our lives. "Thanks, I don't drink!"

23

A Table

GALATIANS 6:2: "Bear ye one another's burdens, and so fulfil the law of Christ."

OBJECT: A table.

ISN'T it a strange thing how much the most ordinary objects that we see all about us every day have to show to us if we just look at them with our eyes wide open? And how much the same ordinary objects will say to us if we just listen to them with care? This morning I want to talk to you about an object that was suggested by one of you when I asked you for your ideas of common objects out of which we could make some of our Children's Sermons. I want to talk about "A Table." Here is one for you to look at. What does it show you as you look with your eyes wide open? What does it say to you as you listen to it talk?

Before we look at the table too closely and before we listen to what it has to say, I want to read you a text. It is from Galatians 6:2; and it says, "Bear ye one another's burdens, and so fulfil the law of Christ."

I

Here is the first thing the table says to us. A good table is usually good to look at. If the table is a good one, it is almost always good-looking. There, for example, is our lovely Communion Table. That's a good table; and isn't it good-looking? I remember the Communion Table in my home Church in Pennsylvania. It was made out of marble from Italy and it had beautiful inlays of sparkling stones that made lovely designs. It was a splendid table and it was handsome to look upon. You all must remember the beautiful mahogany table we have in our Sunday School room. How graceful it is; how beautiful! A table that is really good is usually good to look at.

And boys and girls ought to be, too. They ought to be good and good to look at. The way to do that, of course, is to keep clean and stay bright. The best way to be good-looking, boys and girls, is to have God in you. That will make you good to look at every time. Don't forget it. God in you will make you a beautiful girl. God in you will make you a handsome boy.

II

Now there is a second thing to notice about a table. It must be on the level. For if it isn't, the dishes on it will not hold water, but the water will run out over their sides. The objects placed on the table will slide off. It just will not do the job it is intended for. It won't hold what you put on it. Objects will roll off or slide off and come tumbling to the floor.

You know, on the great ships that cross the ocean, the tables cannot be kept level in a storm. So the men that run the ship and the men who take care of the dining-room put up little board fences all around the edge of each of the dining-room tables to keep the dishes at meal-time from sliding onto the laps of the passengers or onto the floor. So a table, to do its job well, should be on the level.

So should boys and girls. They, too, should be on the level. What does that mean? Doesn't it mean they ought to be honest and true and straight?

III

Now here is a third thing about a table. It is made to hold things. A table will hold a vase with flowers in it. Another table will hold dishes for a meal. Still another, perhaps, papers and books in the library. And another tools in the workroom.

Did you ever think that boys and girls are made to hold things, too? Hold things? What do I mean by that? What are boys and girls made to hold? Information, for one thing. Love, for another.

IV

And there is a fourth thing to say about a table. A table is made to serve people. Now there are two meanings to that word, *serve*. First, it means to provide food, to serve it at the table. Well, a table does that, doesn't it? It helps us serve food to people; it helps us get their food to them; it helps us provide it for them; it gives us a way to get it to them. So a table serves people by serving food to them. But the second meaning of the word, serve, is to help people. And a table certainly does that. All the things that a table is made for; all the things that a table does, surely are helps to people. So a table serves because it helps.

And that goes for boys and girls, too. We should be like a table. Maybe you and I, boys and girls, are not apt to serve people their meals very often. But surely we can help other people. That's a way in which we can be like tables. We can *help other people*. "Bear ye one another's burdens, and so fulfil the law of Christ."

Isn't it funny what a simple, common, ordinary object like a table can show us if we keep our eyes wide open? Isn't it strange how much it will say to us, if we just listen with care?

24

A Chair

GALATIANS 6:5: "For every man shall bear his own burden."

OBJECT: A chair.

OUR text this morning, boys and girls, is found in God's Word as it is written in Galatians 6:5. "For every man shall bear his own burden." Our topic this morning is "A Chair" and there is a chair here for you to look at.

A week or so ago we had a talk on "A Table." And for that talk I used a different text, but one found in the Bible near this morning's text. Then I used Galatians 6:2, "Bear ye one another's burdens, and so fulfil the law of Christ." This morning I am using Galatians 6:5, "For every man shall bear his own burden." The texts are found close together. There are only two verses between them. And the texts are related. And both texts are true. We are to help others. "Bear ye one another's burdens, and so fulfil the law of Christ." We are to help ourselves. "For every man shall bear his own burden." Galatians 6:2 is a good text for a table. "Bear ye one another's burdens, and so fulfil the law of Christ." And Galatians 6:5 is a good text for a chair. "Every man shall bear his own burden." So Galatians 6:5 applies especially, this morning, to a chair and that is what we are talking about and so that is the text we shall think about. "Every man shall bear his own burden." Let us think about a chair.

I

Now a chair must have its feet on the ground. That is the first thing to say. A chair ought to have its feet on the ground. Not on a tight rope. I've seen chairs perched on tight ropes at a circus or a fair; and so have you. But that is not the place for them. That's only a trick somebody is doing to show off. A chair really doesn't *belong* there. And it doesn't belong on another chair, or on a table, or on a shelf. But it does belong on the ground or on the floor. Or at least, on something sure and solid.

And that's the way it ought to be with us. Did you ever hear the saying, "Have your feet on the ground"? It means, have common sense. Be sensible, steady, sure. That's good advice, isn't it? That's what the chair says to us. "Have your feet on the ground."

II

The second thing we notice about the chair is that it must stand on its own legs. A chair is no good if it leans on another, if it cannot stand up by itself. It just can't do its job. It isn't much of a chair.

And so it is with us. We should stand on our own feet. We should do our own job. That's exactly what the text means that I have chosen for to-day. "Every man shall bear his own burden." Look out for yourself. Do your own job. Accomplish your own work. Be self-reliant. Depend on yourself. Stand on your own feet.

III

The third thing to notice about a chair is that it is made for a particular purpose. It is not made to look at. Some chairs are pretty, I'll admit. But they are not made to be admired. And they are not made to pile things on. I do it myself, sometimes, I know. Sometimes I pile books and papers on a chair. And sometimes, in the winter when the snow is deep and the day is stormy, I even pile my coat and hat on top of a chair. Do you ever do that? But that is not what the chair is for. And it is not to be used as a step-ladder, even though many people use it that way. No, a chair is made to sit on. That is its particular purpose.

So we are made for a particular purpose. *God made us to be useful.* We ought to try our best to find out what He wants us to do to-day, to-morrow, and all through our lives. And when we have found it out, we ought to DO IT.

IV

Let us see one more thing about a chair, a fourth thing. We saw something like it about the table. A chair must be on the level, or it just won't hold people, it just won't do the thing it was made to do. The people will all slide off. The chair must be level and straight and firm and solid. It must not rock. It must not sway. It must not tilt.

And that's just as true of us. We, too, must "be on the level." You know what that means, I am sure, for we talked about it last time. It means, Be Square; Be Truthful; Be Honest.

A chair that is not on the level is no good. A boy who is not on the level is no good. A girl who is not on the level is no good.

See what the chair shows us. Hear what the chair is saying.

25

God Needs Your Light

MATTHEW 5:16: "Let your light so shine before men, that they may see your good works, and glorify your Father which is in heaven."

OBJECT: An electric light bulb.

I THINK boys and girls want to be grown-up in Church, like their parents. So I think they ought to have a text for their sermon as their parents have a text for theirs. Our text, then, boys and girls, this morning, is one of the greatest in the Bible, and one of the most familiar. It is found in the Gospel according to Matthew, in the 5th chapter and at the 16th verse. "Let your light so shine before men, that they may see your good works, and glorify your Father which is in heaven."

Many of you will remember when I gave you a talk

on "The Electric Light Bulb." * I used this same text, you probably will remember; and I showed you a bulb like this one, too. And I said that Jesus expected us to shine for Him in the world and to do it we ought to be like an electric light bulb. For if a bulb is going to give off any light it must have four things: a socket; wires running to it; a switch of some kind to turn it on; and power to come over those wires, to be turned on by that switch, to run through that socket and to light up that bulb. And exactly so, I told you, we have to be if we are going to shine for Jesus. We have to have a socket, the place where we are. We have to have wires coming to us, and I called them prayer and the Bible. We have to have a switch, to turn on the light, to make it shine. And I told you that the switch which would turn on the current or the power for us was just to use prayer and the Bible. We have both. To get them to work, we must turn them on, we must use them. And then I said that the power to light up our lives was God. Like a bulb, we must shine where we are; we must be connected to the power by the wires of prayer and the Bible; we must turn on the power by using prayer and the Bible. And the power to make us shine is God Who will come into us and shine through us.

Now this morning I want us to look at the other side of the picture. We cannot shine in the world for Jesus unless God comes into us and makes us shine. But the other side is true, too. How can God shine in the world without us to come into and shine through? How can God shine in the world without *you?* You must have God (that is the power) in you to shine. But there is another side. *God must have you.*

* *A Year of Children's Sermons, Revised Edition,* page 42.

God wants His light to shine in the world. But He can't do it unless He has a bulb to shine through. The power we call electricity that comes over the wires into our houses and our public buildings cannot shine unless it has a bulb to shine through. God wants His glory to shine in the world. But the only way He can do it is through *you. You must let Him use you.*

> Christ has no hands but our hands
>   To do his work to-day;
> He has no feet but our feet
>   To lead men in his way;
> He has no tongue but our tongues
>   To tell men how he died;
> He has no help but our help
>   To bring them to his side.*

God needs your light.

26

The Gospel

JOHN 3:16: "For God so loved the world, that he gave his only begotten Son, that whosoever believeth in him should not perish, but have everlasting life."

OBJECT: A large pasteboard card (the commercial bristol-board, which comes in standard size, 28 x 22 inches, and can be purchased at any stationery store, would be about right) on which is printed, in large letters, the text in the following fashion:

* From *Jesus Christ—And We* by Annie Johnson Flint. Copyright. Reprinted by permission. My hearty thanks to the Evangelical Publishers, Toronto, 1, Canada.

```
For              God so loved
    the          wOrld that He gave
His only
    begotten     Son that whosoever
                              believeth in
Him should
    not          Perish but have

                 Everlasting

                 Life*
```

The six large letters may be printed in red; and also, the six words containing the large letters may be under-lined in red.

⤜⤐

THE text for the boys and girls this beautiful Sabbath morning is John 3:16. "For God so loved the world, that he gave his only begotten Son, that whosoever be-lieveth in him should not perish, but have everlasting life." This is the greatest text in the Bible. It is the best known. It is the best loved. It means the most. It says the most. It is really the Bible in a verse.

Now let us arrange it on a card (display the card with the arrangement outlined above) so that we can all see it, and study it together and get its meaning.

* This or a similar arrangement of the words and letters of this wonder-ful text, John 3:16, to spell out the word "Gospel" and thus vividly suggest the meaning of the text has been used many times before. I have seen it used by evangelists and cartoonists but do not know just where or when I saw it first, and for this reason cannot make proper acknowledgment. The treatment of the text and the application of the arrangement of words and letters in this talk, however, are my own.

I

See the important words in it. They are underlined in red. Let us look at these important words and see what they mean.

1

The text starts with *GOD*. Notice that carefully. The text starts with God. "For *GOD* so loved." God loves us. God gives us all that we have. God provides for us. God takes care of us. That's where the text starts. That's the first important word in it.

2

Next, it deals with the *WORLD*. The world is the second important word in our text and on our card. God loved the whole world. God wants the whole world to be saved. That means, to belong to Him.

3

So He gave His *SON* to do something for that world He loved. This brings us to our third important word, His *SON*. Christ is our Saviour. Christ accomplished our salvation. Christ *did* it for us. Christ died on the cross. God gave His *Son*.

4

That men, if they believe, should not *PERISH*. Here is the fourth word. That men, if they believe, should not *PERISH*. We are hopeless without God and Christ. We are lost. We perish. So, to receive God's gift, we must believe. And if we believe and receive His gift, His Son, we do not perish.

5

Now the gift He gives us is *EVERLASTING*. There is our fifth word. The gift He gives us is *EVERLASTING*. There is no end to it. It is forever ours.

6

And it is *LIFE*. So our sixth word is *LIFE;* real life; abundant life; full life; here and forever!

II

Now, let us take an important letter from each of the six important words. These important letters I have printed in red on our card and have made them larger than the other letters in the words.

Let us take the letter 'G' from the word, 'God.'
And the letter   'O' from the word, 'World.'
And   'S' from 'Son.'
Take   'P' from 'Perish.'
And then take   'E' from 'Everlasting.'
And finally   'L' from 'Life.'

Now, read them together, reading *down* the card, and they spell *GOSPEL*.

That is an old word, and a wonderful word. It means "good news." And isn't this good news? It is the best possible news! "For God so loved the world, that he gave his only begotten Son, that whosoever believeth in him should not perish, but have everlasting life."

27

The Loud Speaker

1 SAMUEL 3:9: "Therefore Eli said unto Samuel, Go, lie down: and it shall be, if he call thee, that thou shalt say, Speak, Lord; for thy servant heareth. So Samuel went and lay down in his place."

OBJECT: A radio speaker of any kind or a horn similar to one.

I WANT to speak to the boys and girls this morning about a radio "Loud Speaker." And I have brought one of these instruments into the pulpit to show you what I mean. I really need not have done that, I think, for you can plainly see that we have two of them on the walls of our Church auditorium. You remember that we have one in the upper Sunday School room and you know that we have one in the Church dining-room. And three large and powerful ones in the Church tower! When I attended the Delaware County Fair a few days ago I noticed that there were loud speakers erected in different parts of the fair-grounds and that from time to time announcements were made over them. Then a few days after that, when I attended the Gouverneur Fair, I observed the same thing. For here, too, at different places on the grounds, loud speakers were erected over which announcements of various kinds could be given from time to time. As clearly as if the speaker were standing next to you, you can hear his voice coming out into the air from one or more of these

speakers or amplifiers as they are called. The whole
thing is called a public address system and is a wonderful way to carry the human voice out over a vast crowd
and over a large space.

We saw a similar arrangement in Potsdam one night
when some of us went over there to hear the famous
Japanese Christian, Kagawa, speak. Loud speakers were
placed at different points in the large hall so that everybody could clearly and plainly hear the great man speak.
And some years ago at Utica I heard President Roosevelt speak from the back end of his campaign train.
And, in spite of the fact that there were thousands
crowding around the railroad station where his train
stopped, we could all hear him very clearly because his
voice was increased or amplified and carried out to the
whole vast throng. The President was standing on the
rear platform of his train and there he spoke. A micro-
phone had been placed before him and the loud speakers were mounted on his car and at various places along
the station platform. That all meant that we could hear
him very plainly indeed.

By such a system, you see, one voice can be heard by
thousands. In our own Church we have microphones in
the organ, before the pulpit, in front of the choir and
in the echo organ. And we have loud speakers in the
tower, in the auditorium, in the Sunday School room
and in the dining-room. So speaking or singing or organ
music or chimes from our organ or records from the
record-player can all be heard from any or from all of
these speakers. And the voice or the music can be carried
to all parts of the Church and out into the air from the
tower.

And the wonderful thing of it is that the voice of a

man can be heard even when the people cannot see the man who is speaking. Just so I heard at the fair that a friend of mine had lost her purse. This announcement came over the loud speakers or the public address system. I thus learned all about it and knew just what had happened although I never saw the announcer who was speaking. To me, the whole thing is wonderful indeed.

But I can tell you something just as wonderful. God can make us hear, too, what He has to say to us. We do not see Him as He speaks to us any more than we see the announcer at the Fair. But He speaks just as loudly and just as surely and just as clearly. Sometimes He speaks to us by our conscience, the voice within us. You have heard your conscience speak to you, many times, haven't you? Well, that is God speaking. Listen to Him.

And then sometimes God speaks to us through history. The way He has dealt with people and nations in the past should be a lesson to us. The way He has cared for America and made it a great and wonderful country should also be a lesson to us. For history speaks to us and when history speaks it is God speaking.

God also speaks to us through nature. A beautiful tree has a message from God. A glistening, brilliant, white star in a clear and cloudless sky on some magnificent night, is God speaking to us.

God also speaks to us through the Bible. On every page of this wonderful Book God has a message for us. Through every page of this magnificent volume God is speaking to us. Listen to Him as He speaks.

And that brings us to our text. 1 Samuel 3:9: "Therefore Eli said unto Samuel, Go, lie down; and it shall be, if he call thee, that thou shalt say, Speak, Lord;

for thy servant heareth. So Samuel went and lay down in his place." The Child Samuel was in the Temple, you remember, working for the old priest, Eli. And in the night he heard a voice and he did not know that it was God calling him. He thought it was the old man, Eli, and he ran to Eli and asked him what he could do for him. But Eli said that he had not called the lad. Three times this happened, you remember, and at last Eli realized that it was God, God in heaven, the mighty Creator of the worlds, Who was thus calling Samuel, His young servant, to follow and obey Him. So Eli told the little boy to go back and lie down again, to listen when the voice came to him and to reply that he was ready to hear and to obey.

And God calls us just as God called Samuel. Not in the same way by a voice in the night, perhaps. But truly just the same, through conscience, through history, through nature, through the Bible. Make sure that you hear Him when He calls. And when you hear God call, no matter how He calls, be sure that you answer Him as Samuel answered Him. Be sure you say to Him what Samuel said, "Speak, Lord, for thy servant heareth."

28

The Musical Tray

(LABOR DAY)

PSALM 90:17: ". . . establish thou the work of our hands upon us; yea, the work of our hands establish thou it."

PROVERBS 31:31: "Give her of the fruit of her hands; and let her own works praise her in the gates."

OBJECT: A carved Swiss bread tray that plays a tune on a concealed music-box when lifted from the table. Or any small music-box. Or any carved article.

❦

IN SWITZERLAND, many years ago, I bought a bread tray. It was made of wood and was hand-carved and very beautiful. I brought it here into the pulpit this morning to show to you boys and girls. It surprises one when it is picked up. (Here, pick up the bread tray or the automatic music-box, if you have one, or the piece of wood-carving.) You see it plays a tune on a concealed music-box the moment you pick it up. That's what makes it interesting. When you pick up the tray to pass the bread to some guest at your table, it suddenly starts to play a tune and everybody is pleased!

You see this tray is so built that it has a little trip on the bottom which is held by a spring against the table on which it is placed. When the tray is lifted, the trip is released by the spring which holds it and it starts the music-box going inside.

Many such articles were sold in Switzerland to tourists before the Second World War; hand-carved articles of all kinds; music-boxes that started themselves; cuckoo clocks, finely and beautifully carved; large and small wood-carvings; pictures and ornaments; all sorts of musical articles. And I suppose that many such articles are being sold there now.

The makers of these articles, the wood-carvers and the clock-makers, the musicians and the artists, are all proud of their work. They make these beautiful things, not only for the money they get out of it. *That is not really important.* They make them also just for the sake of the beautiful piece of work that they can create. They are proud of something well done. They are pleased with the beautiful article they produce.

And *that's the real message of Labor Day,* boys and girls. The pleasure and joy in work that is well done. So the Psalmist said in our first text this morning, Psalm 90:17, ". . . establish thou the work of our hands upon us; yea, the work of our hands establish thou it." There is real pleasure and there ought to be deep joy in work that you do and do well. We ought to be happy over it. We ought to be proud of it. The work that is well done is the important thing, not the pay we may get. We can be proud of something accomplished. We can be happy over something done. So the Book of Proverbs says, in our second text this morning, about a woman's work, Proverbs 31:31, "Give her of the fruit of her hands; and let her own works praise her in the gates." Good work, well-done, praises the doer. "Let her own works praise her in the gates."

So the poet said:

"A thing of beauty is a joy forever." *

29

"Learn of Me"

(STARTING OF SCHOOL)

MATTHEW 11:29: ". . . learn of me. . . ."

* John Keats, 1795-1821: *Endymion,* Book i.

OBJECT: A school book.

❧~~✺~~❧

S CHOOL has started! Here in my hand is a sample of a
school book. All the boys and girls all over the
land are now going to school every day in the week except Saturday and Sunday. School is once more under
way!

We go to school first of all and most of all *to learn*.
That's the reason for school, isn't it? That's why we go,
isn't it? Now I know perfectly well that some of us go
to school for good times. Some go to play football. Some
go just for the school dances. Some of you go chiefly to
see your friends and to have good times with them.
Sometimes there are people who go to school in order to
play in the orchestra and band. Some go, I suppose, to
be in the Senior Play. But the chief reason for going is
to learn.

I

Now it is *important, very important,* to learn to count.
Maybe, when you grow up, one of you will keep store.
All of you will have to buy things in stores. So you must
know that 59¢ plus 21¢ equals 80¢. You must know how
to make and how to count and how to recognize change
from a dollar. Now all of this, and much more, is important. Our teachers call it *Arithmetic*. It is something
we just have to know. We cannot get along very well in
life without it. You cannot sell and you cannot buy if
you do not know Arithmetic. You just have to know
how to handle numbers. It is most important that you
learn how to count.

II

It is also *important* to learn about the world we live in. When you study about the world we live in, we call it *Social Studies,* don't we? Maybe one of you, when you grow up, will work in Syracuse. Well, if you are going to work in Syracuse, you must know *where* it is. Maybe some of you will be farmers. If so, you will have to know how the ground produces crops. Social Studies are important. They teach us something we just have to learn.

III

It is also *important* to learn about nature all 'round about us. This study we call *General Science.* Many things we learn in these classes we just *have* to know. We must know that water runs down-hill. How much trouble we will get into all our lives if we do not *know* and *know that we know* that water runs down-hill. How silly we would be some day if we find ourselves, because we did not learn that simple truth, trying to make water run up a pipe somewhere, or up over a hill on the farm, or up over a roof on a house! We must know that. And we should also know that water will rise in a container or in a pipe only as high as its source. That is to say that water will *run up,* in a closed pipe or container of some kind, just as far as it has been *running down* from the place where it started. Simple, commonplace, ordinary things to know, but very important for us to learn.

IV

And it is *important* to learn to read and to write and even to spell. I suppose we call this *English.* If you are going to have a store or work in an office or labor in a mill or even run a home, you will find that you will just have to write some letters now and then. We call them business letters. And you can't get out of it. You will just have to write some sooner or later. So you ought to know how! You will have to sign receipts, make out bills, sign deeds and do all sorts of things if you are going to make a living and have a home to live in. So you will just have to *learn,* that's all there is to it!

V

So all of these studies are important. But the *most important* of all is to *learn of Christ.* That is certainly the most necessary of all our learning. And that's what our text for the morning tells us. Jesus Christ spoke in Matthew 11:29 and said to us, ". . . learn of me. . . ." That is without doubt the most important learning we can ever get. Let us never forget that! We must learn of Christ.

We should learn Who He is. We should learn what He did for us. We should learn what He is doing for us every day of our lives. We should learn what He will do for us in the future. "Learn of me," Jesus said. Let us learn of Him and we shall have the most important knowledge of all; the knowledge that will make our lives worth while; the knowledge that will make us fine and good and free and happy!

30

A Board in a House

❧~❧

2 TIMOTHY 2:20: "But in a great house there are not only
    vessels of gold and of silver, but also of wood and of earth;
    and some to honour, and some to dishonour."

OBJECT: A piece of clapboard or any other board from a house.

❧~❧

LISTEN carefully, boys and girls, while I read your text
for the morning to you. It is found in the Word of
God, in 2 Timothy, the 2nd chapter and the 20th verse.
"But in a great house there are not only vessels of gold
and of silver, but also of wood and of earth; and some
to honour, and some to dishonour." When I asked for
suggestions from the boys and girls of the congregation
for topics for these talks to the children, one of the boys
requested that I speak on "A Board in a House." So
that's the topic of the talk this morning. "A Board in a
House." Here is a board that came out of a house. It is
a piece of a clapboard, part of the siding with which
the house was covered. It is our object and will help us
think about our subject, "A Board in a House."

Now what is this board saying to us this morning?
What is any board taken out of any house (or still in the
house, for that matter) likely to say to us? It may be a
beautiful board from the peak of the gable in the front
of the house. Or it may be a great beam in the cellar.
Every board in every house has a job to do, a place to fill.

It may be a lovely piece of mahogany over a fireplace. Or it may be a humble piece of oak on a step or in a floor, placed there expressly for people to step on. But the house would not be complete without it. The house would not be beautiful without it. For if the step were missing, the house would be ugly. If the board were out of the floor where it belongs and where it is so necessary the house would not be beautiful for it would be marred. If the piece of ornament over the fireplace were missing the house would be incomplete, unfinished and so not beautiful. Each piece, each board, each part of the house, must be in its place. Each piece must do its work. Each must find the spot intended for it, fill that spot and do its job.

So it is with the world we live in. And so it is with us who live in the world. God has a place for us. That is very true and that is very important. The strange thing is that many of us never knew that. And many of us never find it out. But there is something you ought to know and something you ought always to remember. God has a place for us. *God* has a place for us. God has a *place* for us. God has a place for *us*. I think I have said it enough times for you to remember it. But it's true. And I want you to know it's true.

For some of us, the place God has picked out for us may be a place of fame and honor. We may become famous. We may get high praises. Everybody may know who we are and what we have been doing. On the other hand, some of us may fill a place of importance but one that is not showy. It may be humble but necessary.

The great apostle, Paul, once spoke about the work we do for God and said that each of us had a place to fill and a work to do and that all of us are important.

And he added that the work we do and the places we fill are like a body of a man and the parts of that body. Just as a body has an eye and a hand and an ear, so the thing that we are called on to do may be the work of the eye or the work of the hand or the work of the ear. He said each part of the human body is important, very important. Each part has a function to perform, a job to do, a work to accomplish. If all the body were an eye, where would the hearing be? If all the body were hearing, where would the smelling come in?

And if one part were missing all the body would suffer and be incomplete and unfinished and imperfect. And if one part were hurt, all the other parts would suffer.

And that is exactly the way it is with you and me and our work in this life that God set us into. Our work may be like hearing in the body. We may serve God and other people by being an eye, or a nose or a foot or a hand or a mouth. We may do something, like a hand. We may say something for God, be a mouth. We may go somewhere for Him, be feet. And if one part is missing, if one part does not do its work, if one part is hurt, if one part is lacking, then all will suffer, all will be hurt and the wonderful whole will not be finished or complete or perfected.

FIND YOUR PLACE IN LIFE.

Did you think that this piece of board would be saying all this to us when I picked it up and showed it to you at the beginning of this talk? Well that is what the board is saying, and perhaps a lot more. But especially it is saying this to us, FIND YOUR PLACE IN LIFE.

31

"How Is the Church Coming?"

(RALLY DAY)

❦

MATTHEW 16:18: ". . . my church. . . ."

OBJECT: A cardboard church, such as is furnished by most denominations as a mite box or collection device for Children's Day or Rally Day; or a cardboard cut out of a church; or a picture of a church.

❦

To-DAY is Rally Day in Church and Sunday School and I have a Rally Day text for you. It is one of the greatest and most important texts in the Bible. It is a word of Jesus and is found in the Gospel according to Matthew, the 16th chapter and the middle of the 18th verse. "My church." That is Jesus speaking. And He calls the Church, "My church."

And I have a Rally Day story for you, a true story, the best kind of a story, don't you think? The other day, not so long ago, a small boy met me on the street. He is a member of our Junior Choir and I know him very well, and so do all of you! When he saw me, he shouted, "Hi."

I like that. I like to be greeted by the boys and the girls of our congregation when they see me. For the boys and the girls of the Church are my friends. And I like to be greeted by and to greet my friends. So I answered my little friend right back, "Hi."

Then he asked, "How's the Church coming?"

I like that, too. I think it's a fine thing to show interest in the Church. That little boy proved that he was interested in the Church, what was going on, what the Church people were doing, what was taking place in Church affairs. I am glad people are interested in the Church and what the Church is trying to do and what is going on in the Church. So I was very pleased when my little friend asked, "How's the Church coming?"

Now there's another side to this matter. The Church won't be coming *if people aren't coming to Church!*

How's the Church coming? That's a good question and I am glad people ask it. But you must all remember that *you* make it come along. And it won't come if you don't come!! And if you don't *come,* others won't want to *come!* And the Church will be dead! And that's good advice for grown-ups, too!

You can put it the other way around. To make the Church *go,* people must *go* to Church.

32

What Time Is It?

(WORLD WIDE COMMUNION)

HABAKKUK 2:14: "For the earth shall be filled with the knowledge of the glory of the Lord, as the waters cover the sea."

OBJECT: A globe map of the world.

Our text, boys and girls, for this Sunday, World Wide Communion Sunday, is found in the Word of God, in the prophecy of Habakkuk, the 2nd chapter and the 14th verse: "For the earth shall be filled with the knowledge of the glory of the Lord, as the waters cover the sea." This is exactly the same text that the grown-ups are going to have in a little while when we come to their sermon. And I thought it would be a good text for us, too. "For the earth shall be filled with the knowledge of the glory of the Lord, as the waters cover the sea." This text is slowly coming true. Gradually the earth is coming to be filled with the knowledge of the glory of the Lord. And some day it will be just as full of that knowledge of glory as the waters cover the sea. And one thing that is helping to spread this knowledge of the glory of the Lord over the earth is World Wide Communion.

'Way back in 1936, three men (they were Presbyterians, I think, but that does not make any particular difference) thought of the idea of World Wide Communion. They asked each other why it wouldn't be a splendid idea if Christian people all over the world celebrated communion on the same day. They said, let us start with our own Church. Wouldn't it be a fine thing if Presbyterians here at home, and others clear across the country, say in San Francisco, and still others in mission stations all around the world—in China, in India, in Africa—all had communion on the same day? And so they talked about it and got some churches here and there to try it.

The idea spread. And soon Presbyterians all over the world were doing the same thing; all were having communion on the same day. Soon other churches or other denominations took up the idea. And now, all over the world, all churches, of all denominations, are having communion on this same Sunday. There are a great many in the United States. There are at least three churches right here in our own town of Gouverneur that are having communion this very day, this World Wide Communion Day.

But now, *what is a day?* What is a day, anyhow? Where does a day start? Why a new day starts at the International Date Line in the middle of the Pacific Ocean. At least, that's the way we figure it out so that we can tell time in this old world of ours and so that we can keep the days apart in different regions of the earth. To make it easy for us to tell time all over the earth and to keep the days from getting mixed up here and there, the world has agreed that at this imaginary line that runs through the middle of the Pacific Ocean all of us will understand that a new day starts.

So Sunday came there many hours before it got here. Sunday began at the International Date Line, many hours before Sunday began here in Gouverneur. Because, you see, the day moves around the earth, as the light from the sun moves around the earth. That means that the first Presbyterian Church* to have World Wide Communion on this day is in New Zealand.

Now, suppose, as is very likely, there is a Presbyterian Church in New Zealand which had World Wide Com-

---

* The illustrations in this talk are naturally from Presbyterian churches, the ones the author knows best, but any person in using this theme can adapt his illustrations to fit his own denomination.

munion to-day. And suppose they had it at 10:30 a.m., on Sunday, which is *to-day*. It was really 16½ hours *before* it got to be 10:30 a.m. here. That means it was only 6 o'clock *last night* here when it was 10:30 a.m., Sunday, there. And they had their Sunday service and they celebrated World Wide Communion out there while we were having our supper here last night.

And the day travels around the earth. Let us see what time it was in other places of the world when the Churches out in Wellington, New Zealand, were having Sunday services *to-day* and celebrating communion. And notice the places on the globe as we point them out. When it was 10:30 a.m., on Sunday in Wellington, New Zealand, it was 9:00 a.m., in Sidney and Melbourne, Australia. It was 8:00 a.m., Sunday, in Tokyo, Japan. And it was seven, Sunday morning, in Manila, Philippine Islands. It was six o'clock the same Sunday morning in Chungking, China and in Singapore. It was 4:30 Sunday morning in Calcutta and Bombay; 2:00 a.m., Sunday, in Moscow, Jerusalem and Capetown. It was only one o'clock in the early morning in Rome and in Berlin. And it was midnight, the exact dividing line between Saturday night and Sunday morning, in London. But it was eleven o'clock Saturday night in France and 10:30 Saturday night in Iceland. It was eight o'clock Saturday evening in Rio de Janeiro, six o'clock Saturday evening in New York City and Mexico City, five o'clock Saturday in Chicago, four o'clock Saturday afternoon in Denver and three o'clock in San Francisco. And it was only 1:30 yesterday afternoon, Saturday, in the Hawaiian Islands.

After all, the world is small. Some day Christ will unite it. Meanwhile, World Wide Communion helps.

And at last "the earth shall be filled with the knowledge
of the glory of the Lord, as the waters cover the sea."

SONG OF   MONTH ?

BIRTHDAYS

33

Columbus and the Egg

(COLUMBUS DAY)

O, 1974
4-12 TH
OPENING

ISAIAH 42:10: ". . . the end of the earth . . . the isles, and the
    inhabitants thereof."

OBJECTS: A hard-boiled egg and a globe map of the world.

COLUMBUS DAY comes this week. We celebrate it in
    this country in honor of Christopher Columbus, the
discoverer of America.

I have a Columbus Day text for the boys and girls to-
day. It is part of the 10th verse of the 42nd chapter of
Isaiah. And in this verse the Bible speaks about ". . . the
end of the earth . . . the isles, and the inhabitants
thereof." I think that is a good text for Columbus Day,
for Columbus went to "the end of the earth." He discovered "the isles, and the inhabitants thereof."

Read

There is an old, old story that everybody is supposed
to know about "Columbus and the Egg." It has been
told many, many times. And it may or may not be true.
I am sure I don't know. After Columbus's first voyage
to the New World, he returned to Spain. He had discovered America and so had done a very wonderful

thing. Of course he did not know that he had gone to a new world. He still thought he had sailed to India. But he had proved that the world is round, like this globe map I hold in my hand. And he had sailed part way around it. He thought he had come to India and so he named the people he found here, Indians; and we still call them American Indians. But instead of getting to India, he had discovered America.

Now after his return to Spain, on one occasion, he was the guest of honor at a great dinner party. One of the other guests at the dinner said to him, "Mister Columbus, even if you had not done this great thing, somebody else would. We have many great sailors and smart men in Spain." Remember Columbus was an Italian, but he had sailed to the New World for Spain.

Columbus did not reply. But he took an egg, like the one I hold in my hand, and placed it on the table. Then he said:

" 'Gentlemen, you make it stand here, not with crumbs, salt, etc. (for any one knows how to do it with meal or sand), but naked and without anything at all, as I will, who was the first to discover the Indies.' " *

They all tried. Not one of them could make the egg stand up on the table. At last the egg, having gone all around the table, was passed back to Columbus. He beat it a little against the table and thus crushed one end of the egg a little bit, and it easily stood up all by itself. ". . . wherefore all remained confused, understanding what he meant: that after the deed is done, everybody

* Benzoni: *Historia del Mondo Nuovo,* the first Italian history of the New World, 1565, as translated by Samuel Eliot Morison in *Admiral of the Ocean Sea: A Life of Christopher Columbus.* Boston: Little, Brown and Co., Atlantic Monthly Press, 1942. Page 361. Used by permission and with thanks.

knows how to do it; that they ought first to have sought for the Indies, and not laugh at him who had sought for them first." * After Columbus had made an egg stand up, anybody could do it. After Columbus had found a New World, anybody could do it!

I

Read   Now it was a great thing to discover a New World. It took <u>courage</u>, <u>bravery</u> and <u>faith.</u> Columbus had all three and he had to use all three to cross an ocean which, so far as he knew, man had never crossed before. But he had great courage. He was a man of tremendous bravery. And he had deep faith. So he came to the New World but never knew it was a new world. He died thinking the land he had discovered was a part of Asia and that the islands of the West Indies were islands of Asia. But he gave a new world to mankind. He had discovered America.

And after Columbus had once gotton there, had once come to the New World, had once showed men the route to America, it was easy enough for others to do the same thing. And many others did. For very soon people began coming in great numbers to the newly found lands. Explorers began coming to all parts of the New World. And it wasn't long until people began sailing all the way around the globe! But that's another story!

II

Read   Now as it was with Columbus, so it is with the Christian Life. And that's where the story of Columbus comes

* ibid.

home to us. The Christian Life is a new world, wonderful, glorious, full of charm and joy and happiness.

And it takes courage, bravery and faith to find it. Let us remember that, boys and girls. It takes courage, bravery and faith to find the wonderful new world that is the Christian Life. Believe God. Follow Him. Obey Him. That takes courage, bravery and faith.

And once we get there, once we arrive at Christian faith and life, others will follow us. If we show people the way; if we employ courage and bravery and faith; if we lead into that wonderful new world that is the Christian Life, others will follow us; others will want to come there, too.

O BEAUTIFUL FOR SPACIOUS SKIES

34

Don't Lose Your Bees

(FALL)

p 376 Song of love,

EPHESIANS 4:32: "And be ye kind one to another, tenderhearted, forgiving one another, even as God for Christ's sake hath forgiven you."

OBJECT: A large letter 'B'; either a cut-out, or a 'B' printed on a large card.

OUR text this morning is in Ephesians 4:32, "And be ye kind one to another, tenderhearted, forgiving one another, even as God for Christ's sake hath forgiven you."

On a recent trip in our car to southern New York, Mrs. Schofield and I passed a truck. On it, the driver had several hives of bees. He was probably moving them, perhaps from one farm to another. Maybe they had been sold. Perhaps he was the new owner taking them to their new home. I don't know about that. But there they were, on a truck, being transported along the State Highway, several boxes or hives, homes, where the bees live, you know.

Now it was a beautiful, warm day. And many of the bees were flying around loose. They were all over the road, circling around the truck, flying in and out of the hives and buzzing about all over. One of them even got into our car. And we began to think that the man who was moving those little creatures was surely going to lose some of his bees.

Don't you lose your bees!

Oh! Maybe, you don't have any bees so you are not afraid of losing them. Maybe you have a dog or a cat or some goldfish that you don't want to lose. You probably are afraid of losing them, but you have no worry about losing your bees. Now I am going to tell you something.

There are some "be's"—a different kind of "be's"— that do belong to you. There are some "be's" that are meant for you. You find them in the Bible. And these "be's" that are yours, that do belong to you, are ones you ought to make sure you keep. Don't lose them! Whatever you do, don't lose these "be's"!

What in the world am I talking about? What are these "be's" that are yours and that you find in the Bible and that you ought to keep and never lose? Well, here is one.

I

Ephesians 4:32—"Be ye kind one to another, tender-hearted, forgiving one another, even as God for Christ's sake hath forgiven you." There is one. "Be ye kind one to another, tenderhearted, forgiving one another." We are to be kind and forgiving.

II

And there are other "be's" in the Bible. One is in James 1:22—"Be ye doers of the word and not hearers only, deceiving your own selves." We ought to do right. It is not enough to hear about it. We ought to do it. "Be ye doers of the word, and not hearers only."

III

And here is another one, another Bible "be." Ephesians 4:26—"Be ye angry and sin not: let not the sun go down upon your wrath." There is another "be" for you. "Be ye angry, and sin not: let not the sun go down upon your wrath." That means that when you are angry, control yourself. Don't "get mad" as we say. Don't lose your temper. Don't do wrong. Don't speak evil.

IV

TOUGHEST

And here is still another one, another Bible "be." Matthew 5:48—"Be ye therefore perfect, even as your Father which is in heaven is perfect." Our aim is to be perfect. We are to grow toward that goal. We are to grow and keep right on growing like God. "Be ye therefore perfect, even as your Father which is in heaven is perfect."

And there are many other "be's" in the Bible, lots of

them. We could find a great many if we took the time. But these that I have mentioned make a good starter. Hang on to these. Remember them. Keep them. Don't let your "be's" get away from you!

REV

LAST

35

"Too Much Drinking"

❧❧❧

COLOSSIANS 2:21: "Touch not; taste not; handle not."

OBJECTS: An advertisement for a motion-picture; a wine-glass, a cocktail glass, a coffee-cup.

❧❧❧

THERE is an interesting text in Colossians 2:21. It reads like this, "Touch not; taste not; handle not." When Paul wrote these words at this place, he used them in a different way from the way I want to use them this morning. But they are interesting words and I wish you would think about them with me a little while. "Touch not; taste not; handle not."

After some of us had seen a motion-picture the other night, some one said, "That was a good picture; but there was too much drinking in it." Such a thing can be said of a great many pictures that we see nowadays. Here is an advertisement for a motion-picture. I presume it is a good picture, but I very much fear that there is too much drinking in it. Because, and this is something I want you to notice, to my way of thinking, *any drinking is too much drinking!* And that makes me think of a few things that I should like to say to you.

I

First of all, I want to say that *it is not true that all American families drink every time they turn around.* People who go to see motion-pictures these days would get the idea from many of them that every American family was a drinking family; that it is a regular American custom to serve drinks whenever a visitor comes into a home; that a party cannot be held without alcoholic drinks being served; that everybody is always drinking in every, ordinary, common American home. And so I want to say very clearly and very strongly that it just is not true that all American families drink every time a persons turns around! Nor even *most* American families. Nor even the *average* American family.

Here motion pictures do *NOT* show true American life. Thousands of families in this country *never* drink a single glass of any alcoholic drink. The family I was brought up in *never* did. My own family, here in my own home, *never* does. There are many families in this very Church and many others in this town which *never* drink a single glass of any alcoholic drink whatever. So when the movies give the impression that all American families drink, they are wrong, very wrong, dead wrong!

II

Now there is a second thing I want to say. There is "too much drinking" in many of our motion-pictures. Of course there is, for any drinking is too much drinking! *Any alcohol that is drunk is too much!* I do not care how little it may be. Any alcohol drunk, no matter how little it is, is too much! There is no excuse whatever, *no excuse whatever,* for drinking beverages that contain alcohol, no matter how little, any time, any place, in any manner, for any purpose, for any reason.

Here is where you and I can apply our text and ought to apply our text. "Touch not; taste not; handle not."

III

Here is the third thing I want to say to you this morning. *Don't do something just because others do.* That's the very silliest reason I know for doing something. "Others are doing it, therefore I must do it!" That's no reason at all! Don't do something just because others are doing it. Just because you see it in the movies; just because you see it in other people's homes; just because you see it in public places. Do right; not what others do. Do the right because it is the right. If others are doing the right because it is the right, so much the better. But if others are doing wrong, that's no reason on earth why you should do wrong! Do the right, whether others are doing it or not. Do the right because it is the right. Never do something just because others are doing it!

IV

And here is the fourth thing. *Start the fashion of saying, "No."* Don't be a "Yes man." Have back-bone. Make it stylish to refuse drink. If you happen to sit at a table somewhere with a wine-glass like this in front of you, turn it over or refuse to have it filled. If a cocktail-glass like this is offered you, refuse it. Learn to say, "No," and mean it.

When I was a boy I used to attend Y.M.C.A. suppers back home. And coffee was usually served for the older men present. I got into the habit of turning my coffee-cup over, like this, because as a young boy I did not drink coffee. Grown-ups drink coffee and it does not hurt them, but boys and girls should not. So I turned my coffee-cup down, and some other boys did the same until after a few minutes the whole row at the table had coffee-cups turned down. It would be a fine thing if the custom grew to turn down the liquor glass. And it will grow if you start it and keep at it!

Be polite but be firm. When invited to drink a beverage with alcohol in it, you can say, "Thank you, I do not drink." It would not be out of place to say something even a little stronger than that, "Thank you, I do not drink poison." For that would be telling the truth. Alcohol is poison.

By doing this, we can start the fashion of being right!

As far as liquor is concerned, our text is a good motto: *"TOUCH NOT; TASTE NOT; HANDLE NOT."*

36

The Book That Is Different from Every Other Book

(REFORMATION SUNDAY)

2 PETER 1:21: "For the prophecy came not in old time by the will of man: but holy men of God spake as they were moved by the Holy Ghost."

Objects: A Bible, a schoolbook, a mirror, a cook-book.

To-day is Reformation Sunday, a very important day. On this day the Protestant Church around the world celebrates the anniversary of the Reformation, a very important event. The Reformation gave us many of the most important things that we possess. The Reformation really gave us our liberty. The Reformation really gave us our education. The Reformation gave us our Protestant Church. And the Reformation gave us the Bible.

Now I do not mean that the Reformation invented the Bible or discovered the Bible or made the Bible up. There was a Bible before the Reformation. But very few people had it or were allowed to see it or were permitted to read it and study it. The priests and the very learned men had copies of the Bible. But the common people, the ordinary persons, the every-day families, like your family and mine, did not have it. The Reformation gave the Bible to the people. And that helped change the world!!

Now on Reformation Sunday, I want to talk to the boys and girls a little about the Bible, the great gift which the Reformation gave to the people. The Bible is different from every other book. Here is a schoolbook. Here is a cook-book. Here is a Bible. The Bible is different from all other books. And our text this morning will tell us why. Read in 2 Peter 1:21: "For the prophecy came not in old time by the will of man: but holy men of God spake as they were moved by the Holy Ghost." That's why it is different. It did not come from men, by the will of man. "But holy men of God spake as they were moved by the Holy Ghost." That is why it is different. Men wrote as they were moved by the Holy Ghost. Men wrote as God had them write. God caused men to write it! God moved men to write it! That is why it is different. Let us now notice how it is different.

I

First of all, let us notice its *make-up*. The Bible is composed of 66 parts or divisions. We call them books but they are really parts of the one great, mighty Book. But if you call them books, then you could say that the Bible is made up of 66 books or parts. About 40 different writers wrote those 66 books that together make up the whole Bible. And they were not all written at the same time, by any means. Those 40 different writers lived at different times over a period of some 1600 years. Yet when the Bible was finished, it became a great unity; all parts fit together; every part of it fits snugly into every other part and the whole thing is a single, complete, wonderful, beautiful whole.

II

Let us look next at *its power*. The Bible shows us ourselves as no other book could ever do. We look in the Bible and, behold, there we see ourselves, just as we are. No other book can do this. No other book ever has. No other book ever will. Here is a mirror. We look in this mirror and we see ourselves. The Bible is like a mirror. We look in the Book and we see ourselves.

But that is only part of its power. The Bible also *makes people over*. It changes people. It makes them new. It turns bad people into good people. It turns

sinners into saints. It turns people completely around
and makes them over. It makes them new.

III

The third thing to notice about the Bible is its *un-
changeability*. The Bible does not change. It is the same
to-day as it was yesterday and last week and last month
and last year and last century. It does not change. It is
always the same.

Schoolbooks change. You are not using the same text-
books in school that your older brothers and sisters used
a few years ago or your fathers and mothers used when
they were in school. There is not one book that I used
when I was in High School that is used in High School
to-day.

Stories change. The popular novels that are being read
to-day are not the same ones that everybody was reading
a hundred years ago, or even fifty years ago, or even ten,
or even last year!

Cook-books change. Your mothers do not get their
recipes out of the same cook-books that your grand-
mothers used.

The United States Pharmacopoeia changes all the
time. That's a big name for an important book. It is
the book that the druggist uses to learn how to make up
his medicines. Much of what used to be made into medi-
cine a few years ago is now considered poison and the
recipe book that the druggist uses is not the same one at
all that used to be used.

Books on Science change. The ones that are used in
schools to-day are not at all like the ones that used to
be read and studied. They change every year. They are
always changing.

But *the Bible is the same always.*

IV

The fourth thing to notice about the Bible is its *subject matter*. What is the main subject of the Bible? What does it tell about chiefly? *Jesus Christ*. Some of it was written 1500 years before He was born. Some of it was written 60 years after He was crucified. *Yet Christ is the center and the subject and the meaning of it all.*

V

And the last thing to notice about the Bible is its *Author*. I mean its *true Author*. I told you at the beginning that many men put down the words of the Book into its various parts. But after all, God wrote it! How? By telling men what to write. By keeping them from mistakes in their writing. So God is the Author. God wrote the Book. Thus *IT IS GOD'S BOOK.*

That's why it is different from every other book. *IT IS GOD'S BOOK.*

37

Bells

Exodus 39:25: "And they made bells. . . ."

Objects: Various kinds and sizes of bells to show and ring. I used a tiny harness-bell, a larger sleigh-bell, several small tea-table-bells of china or brass, a large hand-bell such as farm women use to call the men in to dinner, a sheep-bell, a cow-bell, an Indian Temple-bell, a camel-bell from Jerusalem and several others. But any selection of bells would illustrate the points of the talk.

I WANT to talk to the boys and girls this morning about "Bells." The Bible often speaks about bells. For example, our text this morning is from the Word of God, the Book of Exodus, the 39th chapter and the 25th verse. "And they made bells. . . ." Back in Exodus, then, it tells us that they made bells. And we have been using bells ever since.

I

There are many different kinds and sizes of bells in the world. I have brought a few with me into the pulpit to-day to illustrate this talk. Here are some little sleigh- and harness-bells that we hear jingle through the winter. Not so much as we used to, for there are few horses on our roads these days and fewer sleighs. But the tinkle of these sleigh- and harness-bells is a sure sign of winter just the same.

Here is a small bell that we ring at the table when we want the person helping us to come to the table and give us service. People used to use such bells as these very often in the days when all great houses had plenty of servants and families usually had a maid or two to serve the meals. Here is another of a different design. And here is one made of fine china, very pretty to look at and very lovely to hear. Here is another one made of brass and shaped like a little Dutch girl, with a long skirt and the two little brass legs inside the skirt form two little clappers to make the bell ring. Here is another a little larger with a little louder ring; and still another, maybe big enough and loud enough for you to have at your bedside when you are sick and which you can ring vigorously when you want some attention or need some help.

Here are two more. And here is one still bigger and louder, the kind the farmer's wife rings when she wants to call the men in to dinner and the boarding-house proprietor and the country hotel-keeper ring when dinner is announced. Here is a camel-bell from Jerusalem, made of lovely brass, and the clapper is made of a smaller bell hung inside the larger one. Here is one made for use in a Temple in India. This is a sheep-bell. And this is a cow-bell. How well I remember the cows out on the hills when I was a boy in the country. Those cows wandered where they pleased over the old oil-lease that I used to visit as a boy, and each one had a great cow-bell hung around her neck so that the owner would not lose her.

Did you ever see a large bell mounted on a pole outside the back door of a farm-house? I have, lots of times. That bell was a dinner-bell and was rung by the rope that hung from it to call the men in from the fields for a meal. Have you heard the Church-bell ring? Of course you have. And I remember the great fire-bell on the tall fire-house tower across the road from my boyhood home, which rang not only when there was a fire but also every evening at seven-thirty to tell the town what time it was and to announce that the fire-fighters were bedding down the horses, that pulled the old fire-engines, for the night!

Different bells made different sounds. And different bells are made for different purposes.

II

And that's the second thing we ought to say about bells. Let us think for a minute about the different purposes of bells.

"Ring out, wild bells," the great poet Tennyson sang in one of his most famous poems. That poem reminds us that bells are rung on holidays, for that really is a New Year poem and it tells us that we ring bells to welcome the New Year and also for many other national holidays. We also use bells as a call to Church, an invitation to come to God's House and worship Him. A bell is often used as a call to a fire or a disaster. It calls people out to come and help. Often there is a bell to call boys and girls to school.

I remember when I lived in Princeton there was a big Church-bell on top of one of the old main buildings at the University. That bell would ring to wake the students up in the morning and then many times a day to tell them it was time to go from one class to another. And there was another bell just like it over at the Theological Seminary which was rung for the same reasons. But the classes at the University and at the Seminary did not always end at the same time each hour of the day, so that it seemed that there were great bells, like Church-bells, clanging all the time in that old University town.

III

Now what is the point of all this talk of mine about bells? I like bells, I think you can guess this from what I have been saying. But why have I told it to you? Why, here is the point. We are something like bells. We can speak out, like bells. We can say something. We can give a message. We can call to people. And we ought to speak for Christ. There it is. There is the point of my talk. That is why I have been telling you about bells. We, like bells, ought to speak. And *we ought to speak for Christ.*

We ought to do His service. That is what we are put into the world for. There is a different job for each. But we should do His will.

IV

Now there are different things for us to do for Christ. And as each of us does a different thing for Christ, we can be like bells here, too. Different bells do different jobs. We have just been saying that. When different boys and girls do different jobs for Christ they are being like different bells. Thus boys and girls should show the joy of the Christian life. That is being a joy-bell. Boys and girls at times should sound a warning to people. The fire-bell and the distress-bell sound warnings. Oftentimes there are very important warnings that boys and girls ought to sound. Some bells invite people to Church. Boys and girls can invite others to worship. Did you ever think that you could be like a Church-bell? You can, when you invite others to Church and Sunday School. Like a great and wonderful Church-bell, you are inviting people to worship God.

38

You Can Light a Light in China

(MEN AND MISSIONS SUNDAY)

MATTHEW 5:16: "Let your light so shine before men, that they may see your good works, and glorify your Father which is in heaven."

MARK 16:15: "And he said unto them, Go ye into all the world, and preach the gospel to every creature."

MATTHEW 4:16: "The people which sat in darkness saw great light; and to them which sat in the region and shadow of death light is sprung up."

PSALM 67:4: "O let the nations be glad and sing for joy. . . ."

OBJECTS: Four electric extension cords—one short one with socket and bulb on the end to hold in hand; one extending to the end of the pulpit platform with socket and bulb; and one extending to the corner of the Church with socket and bulb. The fourth extension cord, attached to a convenience outlet, must have a three-way connection plug on its end so that the other three cords can be connected to it, one at a time.

I

I HAVE an extension cord in my hand, as you boys and girls can plainly see. It is connected to a floor or wall convenience outlet by means of another cord. On the end of it is a socket, as you can also see, in which is an electric light bulb. This bulb in the socket, which I hold in my hand, will light up when I turn the switch in the socket or screw the bulb into the socket. (Screw the bulb into the socket, or turn the bulb on by means of the switch if socket is equipped with switch.) Now I unscrew the bulb (or snap the button, if the socket is equipped with switch) and the light goes out. You see how easily I can control this light. I can make it light (by screwing in bulb or snapping button switch) and I can turn off its light.

Now notice. I will detach the light in my hand, by pulling its cord out of the three-way connection plug in the end of the extension cord that comes out from the convenience outlet, and in its place will insert the end of another extension cord. When the connection is firmly made, the bulb lights over at the end of the pulpit platform. (Demonstrate.) So you see, by connecting the proper cord, I can light this light in my hand, or I can light the light over at the end of the platform.

Now I will disconnect this second cord and connect a longer one. And a light at the end of the longer cord lights up, 'way over in the far corner of the Church! (Demonstrate.)

I can *stand here,* and by use of one or more extension cords, I can light a light *here*—one at the end of the platform—or one at the end of the Church. (Demonstrate each.) And, of course, if I connect all three at once to my outlet in the end of the original extension cord that runs from the floor or the wall outlet, I can light all three bulbs at the same time!

So the President of the United States sometimes presses a button at his desk in Washington and lights a light for some great fair or some great meeting in San Francisco, New York or Chicago.

I can stand here and light a light clear across the Church, or 'way up in the Church Tower (if I only had the proper extension cords connected up properly) or even miles and miles away!

II

Christ told us to shine for Him. He said so in Matthew 5:16. "Let your light so shine before men, that they may see your good works, and glorify your Father which is in heaven." This we do by being Christians; by acting as Christ wants; by doing Christian things. (Turn on light in hand.) And it is Christ's light that shines in us! His light shines in us. Others see it. They want it, too. Our influence thus goes out. Thus we help others. Thus we help *Him*. So we can shine for Him right where we live, right here at home.

But He tells us to go into all the world for Him. This word of His we read in Mark 16:15. "And he said unto them, Go ye into all the world, and preach the gospel to every creature." We can shine here at home. And we can shine far away. (Turn off bulb in hand. Connect extension cord that lights bulb at end of platform.) Our influence, our Christian living, our Christian deeds, can be seen and felt far away.

We can even shine clear across the world. (Disconnect extension cord to end of platform and connect the one that lights the bulb in the corner of the Church.) We can shine for Christ clear across the world.

III

This is *especially true* in missions. We can shine for Christ at home. (Light the bulb in hand.) By missions, by giving to missions and sending out missionaries who go *for us* and are paid by us, we can shine clear across the United States. For example, Barbara VanSlyke Anderson, a member of our own Church is doing our work and representing us out in Ganado, Arizona, in the Mission School there among the Navajo Indians. She is our missionary out there and through her our light is there shining. Or we can shine even farther than that, even into another country. For example, again, we can shine in the country which is our next-door neighbor, Mexico. (Light the bulb at the end of the platform.) By giving to missions, you see, we can light a light in Ganado, Arizona, or in Mexico.

And also, by missions, we can shine for Christ clear across the sea, half-way around the world. Alexander Reese is the special missionary of this Church in Brazil. And we help support many missionaries in India and Africa and China. We can light a light in China! We can stretch our hands clear across the sea. (Light the bulb in the corner of the Church.) We can stand here at home, give to missions, stretch out our hands, and light a light in China!

So the Bible says (Matthew 4:16): "The people which sat in darkness saw great light; and to them which sat in the region and shadow of death light is sprung up." We light a light. People in darkness see it. They know Christ because we send them the light!

Then the nations of the earth, all peoples, will be glad and sing for joy. Psalm 67:4: "O let the nations be glad and sing for joy. . . ."

You can light a light in China!

39

"What Have I to Be Thankful For?"

(THANKSGIVING)

❧

1 THESSALONIANS 5:18: "In every thing give thanks: for this is the will of God in Christ Jesus concerning you."

OBJECTS: Several old, torn and ragged garments, the older and more tattered they are, the better.

❧

NEXT Thursday, boys and girls, as you all know perfectly well, will be Thanksgiving Day. I have a Thanksgiving text for you this morning. It is found in God's Book, the Bible, in First Thessalonians, the 5th chapter and the 18th verse. "In every thing give thanks: for this is the will of God in Christ Jesus concerning you."

And I have a Thanksgiving story. It is a make-believe story this morning, but the idea in it is true. See if you understand the story and get the true idea that is in it.

Once upon a time there was a boy who was talking to his mother the night before Thanksgiving. He had had a very hard day in school. He had received a low mark in mathematics. He didn't make the basket-ball team. That very day he had been called into the Principal's office and had been severely scolded. The world looked pretty dark to him. Everything was wrong. Everybody was against him. Nothing was right. And so, on the night before Thanksgiving, he complained to his mother and said, "What have I to be thankful for?" He didn't see any sense in Thanksgiving, especially that year. What did it mean to him? What good would it do him? That's why he said sadly and bitterly to his mother, "What have I to be thankful for?"

And so he went to bed. After a long time he woke and discovered that there were no covers over him, and it was a cold night in November, too. My, how cold he was and how he shivered and shook! But then he discovered not only that there were no covers over him, but that he was not even in a bed. He was outdoors; and he was lying on the cold, damp ground; and there was no house about him.

The light came at last and he decided to get up and get dressed. But there were no shoes to wear and there was nothing but some old rags, worse than these I have in my hand, to put around his cold body. But he got dressed as best he could and then hurried off to a town he saw in the distance. But when he walked bare-foot and in tatters and rags into the town he found no school and he saw no friends. Indeed, he did not know one of the men or women he met and not one of the boys or girls would even so much as say, "Hello," to him.

"Maybe Mother is in the Church practicing for the Christmas pageant," he said to himself, almost out loud. He was really beginning to get frightened now. So he looked all around the town, but he could find no church.

"Maybe she has gone to the store," he said, and this time he did speak out loud. But look as he would, he found no paved street; he found no fine brick and stone store buildings. All he could find were straw huts! He looked everywhere, but he really found no store at all. All he could discover were some dirty people in front of a tumbled-down hut trading pigs, chickens, baskets and some blankets for squash, corn and pumpkins.

He went up to a man he saw standing there and spoke to him. He asked the man a question, but the man, for answer, knocked him down. He spoke to another man, and this one kicked him. He went up to a third man and spoke to him, for he was beginning to be terribly afraid by this time. But this man grabbed him, made him carry a live pig, bigger than himself, and beat him with a stick all the time to make him go faster.

At last, hungry and tired and cold and faint, our little boy fell down in the dirty, muddy street. He just could not take another step. He closed his eyes. All was dark about him. He fell asleep, for he was exhausted. He couldn't see. He couldn't think. He could hardly feel. So sleep was a great and a welcome relief.

And then he woke up! And it had all been a dream! He was in bed, his own, soft, comfortable bed. He was as warm as toast. There was a soft blanket over him, as there should have been. The delicious smell of breakfast came up to him from the kitchen below. And he heard outdoors the wonderful sound of the Church-bells ringing for the Thanksgiving Day service.

He hopped out of bed. He jumped into his clothes. He rushed down the stairs. And he called to his mother, "Hurry, Mother, let's eat our breakfast and go to Church. I want to tell God how much I have to be thankful for!"

40

Snow for Christmas

(SUNDAY BEFORE CHRISTMAS)

❧~❧

LUKE 2:10: "And the angel said unto them, Fear not: for, behold, I bring you good tidings of great joy, which shall be to all people."

OBJECT: A globe map of the world.

❧~❧

HERE is your text this morning, boys and girls. Luke 2:10. "And the angel said unto them, Fear not: for, behold, I bring you good tidings of great joy, which shall be to all people." That's a Christmas text, isn't it? Well, Christmas will soon be here. So I have also a Christmas story for you, a true Christmas story. Don't you like true stories best? I think I do.

Well, one day, not so many days ago, either, I was walking along the street in front of the First National Bank. Two boys whom I knew well came along behind me and soon caught up to me and walked a bit beside me. The first boy spoke to me and said, "It's snowing. We're going to have snow for Christmas."

I said in reply, "That's right." And the second boy then said, as boys do, "That's sure right." Then the first boy said something very interesting.

"It wouldn't be Christmas without snow," was his remark.

"But, how about the Hottentots?" I asked him.

"What are they?" he asked me in return.

"Why, the Hottentots," I replied, "are Negroes in Africa, where it's hot and it never snows. Can they have Christmas without snow? They don't have any snow!"

And the boy quickly answered, "No. But they ain't got no Christmas, neither!" Now that was *very bad grammar*. But there is a great truth here. The boy should have said, as I am sure you all know, "They have no Christmas, either." That is good grammar and that is true. That's the truth. They have no snow. And they have no Christmas. That's true enough. But why do they have no Christmas? Not because they have no snow but because they have no Christ!

*   *   *   *

Think! Yes, think that over! If you have no Christ, you have no Christmas. We can have Christmas without snow. People do in Florida and in California, where it is summer all the year. And people do in South America! Did you know that? Let me explain.

South of the equator the seasons are reversed from ours. The people who live south of the equator have winter when we have summer and they have summer when we have winter. That means, you see, that Christmas south of the equator comes in the middle of the summer. Notice how it is on this globe I have here. The month is December and the day is the 25th as it is with us. But December is a summer month south of the equator and July is a winter month down there. So for them Christmas Day comes in the middle of the summer, their summer, not ours, but summer just the same!

We think snow is very important at Christmas time. It certainly is a beautiful, splendid part of Christmas and we are all glad to see it. But we can have Christmas without snow. But we cannot have Christmas without Christ.

*   *   *   *

Christ gave us Christmas because He gave us Himself.

And so we come back to my question, the question I asked the boy on the street who said we cannot have Christmas without snow. How about the Hottentots? They have no Christmas. The boy was speaking truly here. And they have no Christ. That is the sad part of it all. They have no Christ.

We must take Christ to them. Here is the work of missions. Missionaries go all over the world to take Christ to people who have no Christ and so have no Christmas. They work for us, they represent us, they take our place and carry the news about Jesus, the Saviour, to the people all over the world who have never heard of Him and so have never had any Christmas.

Everything you enjoy, except the snow itself, you have because Christ came into the world on the first Christmas. That is something for you to think about. All the things that you enjoy, everything that you feel is valuable and important, all things that are beautiful and desirable, except, as I have said, the snow itself, you have because Christ came into the world on the first Christmas.

Be sure, therefore, that you take Christ to others all over the world. Then they will have Christmas ~~when~~ *Because* they ~~have~~ *will* have Christ!

41

The Christmas Star

(CHRISTMAS)

LUKE 2:9: ". . . and the glory of the Lord shone round about them. . . ."

MATTHEW 2:2, 9, 10: ". . . we have seen his star in the east . . . and, lo, the star, which they saw in the east, went before them, till it came and stood over where the young child was. When they saw the star, they rejoiced with exceeding great joy."

OBJECTS: A star cut out of a board about 15 inches square; a set of Christmas tree lights (not in series, so bulbs can be screwed into sockets and lighted one by one) with their wires tacked on the back of the wooden star so that one socket projects at each of the five points of the star; the front of the star covered with silver paper; a nail or hook placed on the front of the star at each point, to hold cardboard letters; 5 cardboard cards, about 2 x 3 inches each, with letters J-E-S-U-S printed on the cards, one letter to each card; a hole, for hanging on the nail or hook, punched in the top of each card; five red Christmas tree bulbs, fitting the set of Christmas tree lights mentioned above, one in each socket of the five-pointed star, but screwed only part way in so as not to light until screwed in fully in the course of the talk; an extension cord to connect the star to a convenience outlet.

WE HAVE a Christmas text, boys and girls, for this Christmas Sunday. It is really three texts, for it comes from three different places in the Bible, the Word of God.

First I shall read part of the 9th verse of the 2nd chapter of Luke; then part of the 2nd verse of the 2nd chapter of Matthew; and after that, part of the 9th verse of the 2nd chapter of Matthew and all the 10th verse. I will put them all together, and this is what we read. ". . . and the glory of the Lord shone round about them . . . we have seen his star in the east . . . and, lo, the star, which they saw in the east, went before them, till it came and stood over where the young child was. When they saw the star, they rejoiced with exceeding great joy." Do you notice that that text speaks about the glory of the Lord and about a star?

I

Here in my hand is a Christmas star. Let us look at it a little and think about it. For a star is surely a part of Christmas.

One point of this star may stand for *JOY*. (Screw in the bulb at one of the points to light it.) JOY is part of Christmas.

A second point of our Christmas star may stand for *EVERY ONE*. (Screw in the bulb at the second point, being careful to go around the star counter-clockwise, from the speaker's point of view, for easier reading at the close of the talk, from the point of view of the audience.) Christmas is for *ALL*. Surely that is clear. Christmas is not for a few. Christmas is for every one.

The third point may stand for *SUFFERING*. (Screw in bulb at the third point.) You remember that the wicked King Herod wanted the new-born King killed. He did not want any other king in his realm. So he ordered all babies under two years of age in Bethlehem to be put to death by his soldiers. He was not sure just when the King the Wise Men had asked about was born and so did not know how old He might be. So, in order to be quite sure his soldiers did not miss the Baby he especially wanted to kill, he ordered them to kill all the babies under two. There was much weeping and sadness, you see, after that first Christmas, when Jesus was born, even though Jesus was not killed at that time because Joseph and Mary had rushed Him off to Egypt and to safety. And there was other suffering in Christ's life, too, you remember. Christ at last did die, you know, upon the cross. Really He came into the world in order that He might die for us on that cross. He was born to die. He came at Christmas that He might die for us on Good Friday. It may seem hard to understand all this now, but when you are a little older you will see what it means. Meanwhile, I want to remind you that there is much suffering connected with Christmas, and that is why our third point on the star and our third light may well stand for suffering. And there is still much suffering in the world. But Christmas will end it, some day.

Now the fourth point may well stand for *US*. (Screw in the bulb at the fourth point.) We are surely part of Christmas. Christmas belongs to us. Christmas is for us. So the fourth point stands for us. Christ came into the world for US. Christ died on the cross for US. Christ loves US.

And the fifth point may stand for *SAVIOUR*. (Screw in the bulb at the fifth point.) Certainly, one point of the Christmas story has to do with the Saviour. For that is Who Christ is. He saved us on the cross from our sins. He came into the world to be our Saviour.

II

(Now place one of the cards with printed letters at each point of the star, going around the star counter-clockwise, as before, for easier reading, with each letter of the cards showing to the audience as it is hung on the corresponding nail or hook.)

We said the first point of our star stood for JOY. So let us place this card with a 'J' printed on it at that point, where we have already lighted a light, to stand for JOY, the joy of Christmas. (Place the 'J' card on point 1.)

The second point of the Christmas star stands for every one. Let us put this 'E' there under the lighted bulb to stand for EVERY ONE. (Place the 'E' card at the second point.)

'S' is for SUFFERING which we have seen on the star. So we place an 'S' at the third point on the lighted star. (Place 'S' at the third point.)

And 'U' stands for US as the fourth point of the star stood for us. So we place this 'U' at this point. (Place 'U' at the fourth point.)

And 'S' stands for SAVIOUR, so an 'S' ought to be placed at the fifth point of the star, for that point we have said stood for SAVIOUR. (Place 'S' at the fifth point.)

And so we have at the five points of the star these five letters, J,E,S,U,S. And these letters, taken together, spell JESUS. And so we come to the full and final meaning of Christmas.

Christmas means Jesus as our star and our letters say. Christmas is Jesus as the glory from heaven and the brightness of the Christmas star and the meaning of the words all combine to tell us. Christmas is Jesus. Let us not forget!

42

"Only 365 Days till Christmas"

(AFTER CHRISTMAS)

೮ೲ෴

LUKE 2:11: "For unto you is born this day in the city of David a Saviour, which is Christ the Lord."

OBJECT: A calendar.

೮ೲ෴

CHRISTMAS is over. I certainly do not need to tell any boy or girl that! But because we have celebrated Christmas so recently, I think I ought to give the boys and girls a Christmas text to-day, since this is the very first Sunday after Christmas. So I am going to read you a familiar Christmas text, Luke 2:11. "For unto you is born this day in the city of David a Saviour, which is Christ the Lord."

I wonder if you saw some things before Christmas that I saw. Did you see in the newspapers or on signs in the store-windows and other places statements like this, "4 Days to Christmas," "Only 2 More Shopping Days Before Christmas," "One More Shopping Day Before Christmas," and other statements to the same effect? I suppose you did, for such signs were everywhere. And on Christmas Day itself, what do you think I heard on the radio? I heard the announcer say, "Remember, it is only 365 days till Christmas!" Of course, he meant next Christmas! And later on, during the very same day, Christmas Day, I happened to see the blackboard of one of the boys of this congregation. He had written on it: "Just think! Only 365 days till Christmas."

Count it on a calendar, like this one. There are always 365 days from one Christmas to another, unless leap year adds another day. A normal year has 365 days. You know that. A leap year has 366. So there must be at least 365 days between Christmas and Christmas every year!

I

But, really and truly, boys and girls, Christmas is not a once-a-year affair! Now it is true, of course, that the real Christmas happened only once! Christ came into the world once. In one sense, at least, that was the greatest event that ever happened. God came into the world. God became a man. God came to live with us; to show Himself to us; to die for us. So the real Christmas, the original Christmas, the first Christmas, of course, came only once.

II

But the *anniversary* of Christmas will come again, next Christmas. Christ's birth into the world happened only once, of course. But the *anniversary* of His birth comes every year. So there will be another *anniversary* of His birth next Christmas. It is just like you. You were born only once. But you have a birthday, an anniversary of your birth, once a year.

III

The whole world was changed because Christ came. It was never the same again and never will be the same again. Hope and love and light and music came into the world when Christ came. Fear and hate and sin and trouble all began to be destroyed. We live in a different world because Christ came, because He was born into this world, because of Christmas.

IV

And so we ought to act every day as if Christ were here. For really He is here, at our side! Christ is with us. Christ is beside us. Christ is at our side all the time.

Some people have on their walls at home a motto which reads:

> Christ is the Head of this house,
> The unseen Guest at every meal,
> The silent Listener to every conversation.

Christ is here, always! We should act as if we knew it!

V

And Christ is coming again! That is a fact we ought always to remember. Christ is coming again. Not as a little baby. Not poor and humble. Not in a stable. But as Judge and King and Ruler of all the earth! Christ should be in our hearts all the time. But more than that, He is coming to judge and to rule the whole world in glory some day. When we think of His first coming, at Christmas, we should also think of His second coming, in glory.